# Mr. Hockey

# Mr. Hockey

## Gordie Howe

### My Story

G. P. Putnam's Sons

New York

PUTNAM

G. P. PUTNAM'S SONS
*Publishers Since 1838*
Published by the Penguin Group
Penguin Group (USA) LLC
375 Hudson Street
New York, New York 10014

USA • Canada • UK • Ireland • Australia
New Zealand • India • South Africa • China

penguin.com
A Penguin Random House Company

Photo credits:
2011 Hall of Fame Inductee Mark Howe with Gordie: Matthew Manor/Hockey Hall of Fame;
Gordie Howe playing for Whalers: Lewis Portnoy/Hockey Hall of Fame; Gordie Howe injured on
ice: Hockey Hall of Fame; Gordie Howe delivers elbow: CP PHOTO/Doug Ball; Gordie Howe
shooting for Detroit: Hulton Archive/Getty Images; Gordie and the Stanley Cup–winning Red
Wings: Courtesy of the Detroit Red Wings. All other images courtesy of the Howe family.

ISBN 978-0-399-17291-5

Printed in the United States of America
1 3 5 7 9 10 8 6 4 2

Penguin is committed to publishing works of quality and integrity.
In that spirit, we are proud to offer this book to our readers; however, the story,
the experiences, and the words are the author's alone.

*For Colleen, the love of my life,*
*and for my children,*
*Marty, Mark, Cathy and Murray*

# CONTENTS

# FOREWORD
# BY BOBBY ORR

**M**any times over the years, I have been asked who I consider to be the greatest hockey player of all time. My answer has never changed—it is Gordie Howe. And so, being asked to write a foreword for Gordie Howe's memoir is a great honor for me.

I'm not sure that younger generations of sports fans realize just how good Gordie Howe was as a hockey player. Certainly, people know he is one of the legends. I observed that firsthand when he attended a Canucks–Sharks game in 2013. When the TV cameras spotted him and put his face on the Jumbotron, the place erupted in a spontaneous standing ovation. Players from both teams stood at their respective benches, everyone reluctant to line up for the face-off. So, yes, there is a healthy respect for Number 9.

But I'm not just talking about being *one* of the greatest hockey players ever. I am talking about being *the* greatest player ever. Period.

Think of it this way: Today, if a player cracks the top five in scoring in the NHL, he's considered a star. Do it a couple of years in a row and you're a superstar. Alex Ovechkin did it once. Sidney Crosby has done it back-to-back twice. Steve Stamkos managed it four years in a row. You get the idea. You have to be a pretty good hockey player to make that list even once. Well, Gordie Howe did it *twenty years in a row.* That's right—*twenty.* How do you begin to do justice to a legacy like that? Maybe we should compare him to the greats in other sports. When you look at golf and the way in which that game celebrates legends such as Arnold Palmer and Jack Nicklaus, you get a sense of what Gordie Howe means to hockey.

Gordie is a quiet and humble man. But I don't think I've ever met anyone with a more determined will to win. If you ever watched him in action during his career, you know that it's hard to describe how he could dominate. We're all taught to play with both hands on our stick. Gordie must have missed that day in hockey school, because he was happy playing with just one. When I came into the league, one thing I noticed after making the jump from junior was just how strong the guys were. And there was Gordie: stickhandling and passing with one hand and pushing the best players in the world off with the other hand. If Gordie wanted to hold on to the puck, there was pretty much no way you were going to get it.

Hockey fans often wonder what would have happened if Gordie had been in the lineup for the 1972 Summit Series against the Russians. The series came during his first retirement, but I would have liked to see what he did on the ice. Would the Russians have found a way to defend against him? No one in the NHL ever did. And when I say "ever," I'm talking about more than twenty-five years. No doubt about it, Gordie would have made Canada a better team.

Coaches usually come up with a game plan to contain the stars on the other team, but there was really no way to contain Number 9 completely. That kind of coaching requires you to identify a weakness, and Gordie didn't have one. What was there to exploit? He could play along the boards with the very best. He could dangle in open ice as well. Try to stand him up and he'd knock you down. Outmuscling him was never going to work. You could try to pressure him, but there was hardly a cooler passer in the game. How do you defend against all of that? One thing you didn't want to do, though, was try to get under his skin. That approach can work against a lot of star-quality players. If you're "the man," guys are going to take liberties with you. Gordie was definitely the man, but after a while even the toughest guys in the league knew not to stir up the hornet's nest. If you got under Gordie's skin, you would soon wish you hadn't. I say this as someone who once got his stick up a little too high on Mr. Hockey. Not long after what he considered to be a cheap shot, I found myself on my rear end with Gordie looking down at me, a very unfriendly expression on his face. When I asked him about it later, he showed another side of his personality—his sense of humor. "I'm a very religious player," he said. "I think it's much better to give than to receive." Not too many guys made that mistake twice with Number 9.

We talk about the role of the "enforcer" in the game, but Gordie didn't need one. He wasn't just an elite talent, but was something of an enforcer himself. He would stick up for himself and his teammates. Gordie eventually had some teammates he took special care to protect. Playing with his sons Mark and Marty meant that a whole new generation of opponents had to learn to be careful around anyone with "Howe" on the back of his jersey. A father and two of his boys playing professional hockey at the same time on the same team . . . I wonder if that will ever happen again!

After I retired from the game, Gordie was still playing and doing it well enough to be voted onto All-Star teams. Here's a little history for you: He played in his first All-Star Game in the year I was born. He retired and had been inducted into the Hall of Fame but then returned to the game, still producing nearly a point a game while playing in the NHL. In 1980, the All-Star Game was held in Detroit. Naturally, Gordie was chosen to represent Hartford that year. In many ways, he was a sentimental favorite. Incredibly, that was his twenty-third All-Star Game while playing in his fifth decade as a pro, an unheard of statistic. The average NHL career lasts about five years. And keep in mind that the *average* NHL player is a very good hockey player. That means that Gordie had greater than four times more All-Star seasons than most very good players have seasons, period.

Now, there he was, back in Detroit where he had started playing in the 1940s. The fans went crazy. One by one, players were introduced as they came onto the ice. As future Hall of Famers like Larry Robinson, Darryl Sittler, and Guy Lafleur came skating out, the announcer called out their names and the teams they were representing.

Then it was Gordie's turn.

"From the Hartford Whalers, representing hockey with great distinction for five decades, *number 9 ...*"

The announcer never got to say Gordie's name. Everyone in Detroit knew who wore number 9. The fans at Joe Louis Arena were on their feet before the announcer had finished, and they remained standing while Gordie stood on the blue line. You could tell he wasn't sure what to do. He would look up and the crowd would roar. Then he would look back down. He wasn't comfortable being the center of attention. But the cheers went on and on. Then the chant went up: *"Gordie! Gordie!"* Finally, after several minutes of this deafening roar, the officials were able to have the anthem played in order to start the game. By the way, at the age of fifty-one, Gordie had an assist in the game.

As I consider his wonderful career today, I realize that Gordie's accomplishments are so impressive that it is almost impossible to understand them by comparing them to those of other players. You can't say that he played like this guy or that guy, because there has never been anyone who played the total game in the way Gordie did. No one has ever combined strength, skill, determination, and longevity in the way Gordie did over all those years. No one captured the respect of players and the adoration of fans like Gordie did. And no one handled that level of fame and stardom with such genuine humility and graciousness. Even today, he still greets fans with the kind of warmth you just can't fake. So you can't talk about how great Gordie was as a hockey player without also mentioning what a great person he is.

His longevity as a professional hockey player reflects his absolute passion for the game. I believe it was his passion to play that set him apart from his peers. As a young teenager, meeting Gordie for the first time, I already knew he was special. That feeling has not changed. Gordie Howe will always be one of my heroes. And, in my opinion, he will always be the best that ever played.

*Bobby Orr*

# INTRODUCTION

The puck felt good in my hand.

I'd have liked it to be on my stick, but I suppose those days are long past. The only time I get on the ice now seems to be when I'm part of an occasion, which is exactly where I found myself last New Year's Eve. Detroit was hosting the 2014 NHL Winter Classic, an outdoor game between the Red Wings and the Maple Leafs. The next day, more than a hundred thousand people would turn up at Michigan Stadium to watch Toronto beat Detroit in a shootout. But New Year's Eve was for the old-timers.

The Wings had asked my old linemate Ted Lindsay and me to drop the ceremonial first puck in an alumni game between the two clubs. Steve Yzerman, retired since 2006, looked like he could still be playing in the NHL as he lined up to take the draw against Leafs captain Darryl Sittler. The weight of the rubber puck was pleasing as I bounced it in my hand and waited for them to come to the circle. I glanced over at Ted, as I had so many times before, and it seemed like it hadn't been that long ago that we'd lined up to take the draw for real. We've both added more wrinkles and our hair is thinner, but he didn't look that much different to me than when we were on the Production Line together.

More than thirty-three thousand fans had shown up at Comerica Park, the Tigers' home field, to watch hockey. I've been around Detroit so long that I can remember taking batting practice in old Tiger Stadium, when it was still called Briggs Stadium. As much as things change, though, they also stay the same. Hockey, for one, has remained a constant in my life. It doesn't matter whether I'm in an NHL arena, at a local rink, or on a sheet of ice in the middle of a baseball stadium, when I'm around the game I feel at home. It's a good thing, too, since I was such a shy kid. No matter how many people were in the stands, though, nerves were never a problem for me when I played. The ice was the one place I always felt comfortable. Stepping in front of a packed house at Comerica Park, I found that what was true then still held true that day. The faces may have changed, but when I waved to the crowd, it felt as familiar as if I were back at Olympia Stadium. I'm lucky for that. I'm lucky in a lot of ways.

I was fortunate enough to play professional hockey for thirty-two years. If you'd asked me when I broke into the league if I thought I'd still be playing five decades later, I would have said you were crazy. When the Red Wings called me up from their farm club in Omaha in 1946, I just wanted to last the season. From then on, if the team decided to bring me back for another year, I wasn't going to complain. From the time I was a kid, all I ever wanted to do was play hockey. Even at the end of my career, when I was the only guy in the dressing room with grandkids, strapping on my pads every day still felt as normal as ever. The air turning chilly in the fall was like nature's way of telling me to put on my skates and get back to work.

I ended up watching a lot of the world go by while on the ice. My NHL career started a year after Harry Truman replaced Franklin Roosevelt in the White House. When I retired, Ronald Reagan was only a year away from taking over from Jimmy Carter. In between, I saw seven American presidents pass through office and even had a chance to meet some of them. It was a good long run by nearly any measure. During my first season with the Red Wings, Jackie Robinson was still a year away from breaking Major League Baseball's color barrier. When I hung up my skates for the first time in 1971, he'd already been in the Hall of Fame for a decade. In Detroit, we had front-row seats for the birth of Motown. I moved there during the city's boomtown years, when Michigan was the center of the U.S. automotive industry. On the ice, the Red Wings piled up four Stanley Cup victories, and we probably should have won a few more. I managed to put the puck in the net 975 times in my professional career, while setting up scores for teammates on more than 1300 other occasions. Away from the arena, I was lucky enough to meet my beautiful wife, Colleen, and together we raised four wonderful children.

I like to think that I'm a family man first and a professional athlete second. With that said, though, I also know that I have hockey to thank for so many of the good things that have happened to me over the years. The game has blessed me with a lifetime of memories. I've had a chance to share some of them before, but I've never taken the time to tell my whole story in one place. It's humbling to think that a shy kid from Saskatoon could write a book that anyone would want to read. As with so many things in my life, I'm grateful—and still somewhat amazed—to be given the opportunity.

S ince retiring, I've often thought that some of the happiest years of my career were spent in Houston, where I had the chance to play with my sons Marty and Mark. I wasn't the player then that I was during the glory years in Detroit, but how many fathers get the chance to play professional hockey with their kids? It's what brought back the fun and excitement of my youth and kept me going into my fifties. Standing rinkside at the Winter Classic watching Mark—who's best remembered as a Flyer, but ended his career in Detroit—take the ice for the Red Wings, it was easy for me to recall our years playing together in the World Hockey Association. Now retired for nearly twenty years and nursing a couple of bad disks in his back, I thought Mark still looked as smooth as ever on the ice. The countless laps he put in skating around the rink as a kid were clearly enough to last him a lifetime.

The alumni game, as exhibition matches often do, started slowly. Time away from the ice combined with a windy day and below-freezing temperatures had everyone more concerned about staying warm and healthy than trying to make a big play. Both squads were filled with players who knew each other well. The Leafs had brought fan favorites such as Doug Gilmour, Wendel Clark, and Borje Salming, while the Red Wings had matched with stalwarts like Brendan Shanahan, Igor Larionov, Sergei Fedorov, and Nick Lidstrom. Everyone was happy to laugh with old teammates and share a smile with former rivals—at least at the start of the game.

Compared to my era, NHL hockey has evolved in ways that are both good and bad. When I watched the alumni game, it was comforting to see that at least one thing hasn't changed: The will to win never goes away. The boys on the ice may have lost a few steps, but once they'd warmed up, they couldn't help themselves. It didn't matter how long they'd been retired, who they were playing, or where the game was being held—no one wanted to lose. At one point, Tiger Williams even started chirping at Chris Chelios for celebrating a goal with a little too much gusto. He wasn't kidding, either. I might have some quibbles with the way the game is played today, but at its core, I know that hockey will always be hockey no matter what year the calendar reads.

Today's brand of NHL hockey is still exciting, but if I had my way I'd like to see more creativity come back into the game. When I played, there were more opportunities to carry the puck, but you don't see that as much anymore. As the game has evolved, the schemes have become more sophisticated. My old coach Tommy Ivan used to say there were only two moves you needed to know in order to play defense: either you knock the puck away from the man or you knock the man off the puck. It worked for us in the 1950s, but the game has changed a lot since then and, unfortunately, not all for the better. I don't need to rehash criticisms of the neutral zone trap and other systems used to slow down talented players, except to say that they've choked some of the excitement from the game. These days, offenses are often reduced to dumping the puck into the other team's zone or chipping it off the boards. There's not enough room for players to generate speed through the neutral zone and make a play. This isn't to say that the game isn't good; far from it.

The NHL used to be limited to Canadian and American players, but now it includes the best players from around the world. I thought about that at the alumni game while watching Mark take a shift with Slava Fetisov, his old defense partner. Slava was there along with the other members of the so-called Russian

Five—Igor Larionov, Slava Kozlov, Sergei Fedorov, and Vladimir Konstantinov—who played together in Detroit in the 1990s. Seeing Russians and Europeans in the NHL is commonplace now, but it still feels relatively new to players of my generation. It's made the game better.

When I'm asked to compare players from different eras, my answer is always the same. I'm convinced that great players would fare well no matter when they played. If Sidney Crosby had been around in the 1950s, he'd have been as good then as he is now. Likewise, Maurice Richard, Bobby Orr, and Wayne Gretzky would be standouts in any era. As for Gordie Howe? Well, my sons figure I'd do well in today's game provided I could figure out how to stay on the ice. I was fortunate enough to win a number of awards during my career, but the Lady Byng Trophy wasn't one of them. That wasn't an accident.

To my way of thinking, the two most important things you need to survive in pro hockey are time and space. I found that a surefire way to earn a wider berth the next time I came around was to give someone a good crack. If his teammates took away a message as well, then so much the better. I'm aware that not everyone approved of how I played, but I don't think any apologies are in order. Early in my career I decided that it was worth it to do whatever was necessary to earn the extra split second it takes to make a pass or shoot the puck. The way I saw it, everyone in the league was getting paid to do a job. Mine was to help my team win games. There were lines I wouldn't cross, but as long as I did everything in my power up to that point, I didn't have any problem sleeping at night.

These days, officials might see things differently. Back then, we had more leeway to police ourselves, and I think the game was more civilized as a result. Everyone knew the rules, both written and unwritten, as well as the consequences for breaking them. It bred a lot of respect into the game. The referees still blew their whistles, but the play wasn't stopped as often as it is now. Of course, today's game also has its advantages. In my day, there was too much hooking and holding by players who couldn't keep up. It was terrible. The league has done a good job of cutting down on much of that nonsense. I enjoyed the style of hockey played in my era, but I suppose there will always be trade-offs no matter when you play.

Since retiring, I'm sometimes asked how I managed to play into my fifties. My answer is simple: I loved playing the game. That's all there is to it. It's the one thing I have in common with every great player I've ever known. It doesn't matter who you ask—Maurice Richard, Jean Béliveau, Bobby Hull, or Bobby Orr—the answer is always the same. I remember being at a banquet in Brampton in the early 1970s and meeting an eleven-year-old Wayne Gretzky, who was already making a name for himself by that point. When I shook his hand, I saw a look in his eye that I recognized straight away. Years later, I wasn't the least surprised when his name started going into the record books.

If I learned one thing by playing professional hockey for thirty-two years, it's that you have to love what you do. And that's not just true for sports. Not long ago, I was talking to our son Murray, who's a doctor, and told him the same thing. If a day comes when he wakes up and doesn't love medicine, then he'll know it's time to hang up his lab coat and do something else. It wasn't the first time we've had that conversation and it probably won't be the last. I figure life's too short to live any other way.

I was lucky enough to find hockey when I was six years old. It's been eighty years since then, and I still love the game just as much as I ever did. I don't have to scratch very far beneath the surface to find the shy kid who was raised in Saskatoon in the Dust Bowl years. Looking back at where I've been still makes me shake my head in disbelief. I couldn't have been any more fortunate. I wish everyone my kind of luck.

*One*

# EARLY DAYS

H ow do I even begin to tell the story of my whole life? Like so many folks, I've been a father, a son, a friend, and a husband. I've done things I'm proud of and some I wish I could take back. And, of course, there's hockey. For the Howe family there's always hockey. I love the game. It was good to me, and when I stop to think about it, I like to believe I gave a little back to it as well. One thing is for certain: I never got tired of lacing up my skates. If I could take a few turns around a sheet of ice right now, I would.

As much as I'm known for playing hockey, the game isn't where my story starts. In fact, it doesn't even begin with me. The whole thing was set in motion long before I even showed up. It's humbling when you stop to think about it. If you make it anywhere in life, you owe that success to the people along the way who stuck up for you, or made sacrifices for you, and gave you a push when you needed it. In my case, those people were my family.

In any case, to tell the story right, I need to go all the way back to the beginning—to a little farmhouse with a dirt wall in Floral, Saskatchewan. People often assume that I come from Floral, but that's not exactly right. I was born there on March 31, 1928, but nine days later the family moved down the road to Saskatoon. There wasn't much to Floral back then. Just a small collection of houses huddled around a grain elevator. I went back to see our farmhouse once. It was a few miles from the elevator, tiny, made of wood, and built into a hill. I thought about my parents living in such a dingy place, raising a bunch of kids. The high plains of Saskatchewan can get pretty bleak, especially during winter. Their lives weren't easy; I know that.

My father, Albert, or Ab, came to Canada from Minnesota, lured by the promise of a homestead under the Dominion Lands Act. He did his best as a farmer, but growing crops on the Canadian prairies at the start of the Great Depression wasn't a guaranteed way to feed a family. To help make ends meet, he would pick up work as a mechanic at a local service station or on construction sites. That's where he was when I was born. He'd taken his horse team into Saskatoon, about nine miles west, to work as an excavator.

My mother, born Katherine Schultz in Stuttgart, Germany, was the strongest woman I've ever known. When she was young, she was separated from her parents and was passed from family to family until her grandfather found her. He was a coffin maker and often buried victims of cholera, typhus, and influenza. People would knock on his door and hand their dead children to my mother, who was little more than a child herself at the time. My mother came from tough stock, to say the least. She eventually reunited with her family and later immigrated with them to Canada. They ended up in Windsor, of all places, right across the river from Detroit. Mum took a job there as a housekeeper until her family decided to move farther west. That's how she ended up in Saskatchewan, which is where she met my dad. On the day I was born she was outside chopping wood when her labor pains set in. At that time, pioneers often had to take care of themselves. I was the sixth of nine children, so she knew what to do. With only a couple of kids around for company, she put some buckets of water on the stove and got into bed. After I was born, she cut the umbilical cord herself and waited for my father to come home. As I said, Mum was tough.

She wasn't doing so well when Dad finally arrived, so he hurried over to my Aunt Mary's place and brought her back to look after Mum. She'd been hemorrhaging from the birth, but she healed up pretty quickly after she got some proper care. In the meantime, Dad, who'd given up on trying to scrape out a living off the land, packed up the house in Floral and moved the rest of us into a place on the outskirts of Saskatoon.

In those days, we didn't have a lot; no one really did. Dad was always hustling around for work, picking up this job or that one. Eventually he was hired as a foreman with the city and he ended up working there for as long as I can remember. To make ends meet, Dad used to do some hunting. The government would pay a one-cent bounty for gopher tails and you could get up to $15 or $20 for a coyote pelt.

My father was a real outdoorsman and he could ride a horse with the best of them. He used to talk about a roan he had once. It was known as a killer horse—it would kill a man if given the chance—but it could really run. Its owners wanted to put it down because it was too dangerous, but Dad stepped in and said he'd take it instead.

One time, before I was born, he was out in the countryside on that horse looking for work and saw a coyote. The way he told the story, he couldn't shoot it because he couldn't afford any cartridges for his rifle, but the coyote was too valuable to let go. He spurred that horse and they took off after the coyote. After a long chase, they ran the thing down. Since his gun was useless, my father took out his hunting knife, leaned over in the saddle, snagged the coyote's back leg, and slashed its tendon. Then he dismounted and finished it off. He took the coyote to the factor, got paid, and had enough to buy more ammunition. That was the type of guy Dad was. He did what had to be done to get by.

There were eleven of us in that little house in Saskatoon: my parents and nine kids, four boys and five girls. I was pretty much in the middle: Gladys, Vernon, Norman, Violet, Edna, me, Victor, Joan, and my little sister Helen.

When we were kids, we didn't have a lot. I guess we were poor, but we never really thought about ourselves that way. It was just the way things were. Of course, they were that way for a lot of families. I won't go into the history of the Great Depression, but those were tough times. Between low grain prices and terrible harvests, farmers were taking a beating. Farms were abandoned all over the Prairies, and there was a steady stream of people leaving in the hopes of finding work somewhere else. Sometimes we'd eat oatmeal two or three times a day because that's all my parents could afford. For milk, my dad used to buy Carnation powder and we'd add about a gallon of water to it. If you've never tried watered-down powdered milk before, I don't recommend you start now.

The lack of proper nutrition eventually caught up with me. When I was just a kid, the doctor told my mother that my back wasn't strong enough and I was developing spinal problems. He said that if I fell down or took the wrong kind of hit, a hard enough blow to my back might break it. He put me on some vitamin supplements, as well as on my first physical training program. It was sort of like a homemade version of the physiotherapy we have today. He had me hang like a monkey from the top of a doorway and swing my hips from side to side. The idea was to strengthen my back muscles and straighten my spine. It was pretty crude but it must have worked. My old back held up through more than thirty years of professional hockey, so I guess that doctor knew what he was doing.

From a certain perspective, I suppose I could say that I have the Great Depression to thank for jump-starting my hockey career. It was 1933 and we weren't the only family in Saskatoon that needed a few extra dollars. One day, a neighbor whose husband was sick came to the door with a gunnysack full of her used things and asked my mother if she would buy it to help the woman get milk for her family. Mum didn't have much, but she was able to scrape together a few dollars. That's the way things were then. When the going got tough, sometimes it was neighbors looking out for each other that allowed everyone to get by. Like so many things in my life, I have my mother's kindness to thank for what came next.

We dumped out the sack on the floor and, along with some old clothes, out came a pair of skates. I spied them immediately, but so did my sister Edna. She grabbed one, I grabbed the other, and we ran outside to try them out. They were a men's size 6, so we pulled on a bunch of woolen socks to get them to fit. We had patches of ice in the garden out back where the snow would melt and then freeze. Edna and I started pushing ourselves across this ice on one skate each. We'd run like hell, pick up our socked foot, and glide across the ice.

When we talked about it years later, my mother and I recalled what happened next differently. She told me my sister kept her skate for a week. I wanted it badly, but she wouldn't let it go. Eventually I broke down and offered her a dime for it, which Mum loaned me, and Edna finally let me have it. What I remember is my sister getting cold after a few nights of skating and going inside to warm up. Once she took off that skate, I snatched it up and that was the last she ever saw of it. Whichever way it happened, I know that putting on those skates was the moment I fell in love with hockey.

From that day on I skated for as long as I could, whenever I could. I don't know if it was because I thought I could do well at hockey or whether I just loved to skate. I do know that whenever I jumped on the ice, I felt like a million bucks. Later on, when I got a bit bigger, skating was the thing that really opened up my little world.

Back then, if we had heavy rains or an early snowfall, the water would collect in the gullies and sloughs and ponds. When winter came and the water froze, we would get great patches of ice all over the place. The Hudson Bay Slough was about three blocks from my house. We'd walk over there, jump on it, and skate forever. It ran for about four miles, nearly out to the airport, and we'd skate the whole thing.

We also knew where to find all the best skating ponds. All you'd need to do was look for the bluffs on the landscape. Most of them had ponds in between them, so we'd go up into the hills, look down, and there'd be a nice sheet of ice just waiting for us. We'd play until we cut it up; if the ice was thin, it might get a little rubbery and the water would start to follow your tracks. Then we'd take off our skates and move on to the next pond.

When winter really set in and the river froze, we'd play on it as well. The Prairies can get pretty windy, which isn't much fun most of the time, but it did clear the snow off the South Saskatchewan, the big river that flows through Saskatoon. It felt like we could skate on it all the way to the next city if we wanted to. Mostly, though, we'd make our way up to the Grand Trunk Bridge, a big steel trestle railway bridge that's still there. The ice was good under that bridge, as a rule, and we used to play hockey in between the piers.

When I first started out, my dad used to sharpen our skates with a file. After a while that became a lot of work, so he came up with a pretty ingenious invention. He was always handy as a mechanic and he built a contraption that hooked on to the washing machine. Then he attached a belt to the flywheel of the washer that turned a grinding stone. After that he was able to sharpen our skates all the time without much fuss.

The ice we used to skate on really put Dad's homemade sharpener through its paces. The gravel roads in Saskatoon at the time had four ruts in them for car tires. During the day the snow that covered the roads would melt slightly, and then at night it would refreeze, which created ribbons of ice that were just made for skating. I even had street shoes with blades on them. The odd time that I'd get a new pair of shoes, my dad would take the old ones and attach metal straight blades to their soles. They made great skates. As soon as he put the blades on, I'd be off. The whole city was like our backyard. We could go anywhere we wanted, and we did. We'd even get behind a bus, grab on to the bumper, and go for a free ride. We called it "trailing." The drivers weren't too happy about it.

Every now and then they'd stop and chase us, but it wasn't much of a deterrent. We could skate faster than they could run, so it wasn't like getting caught was a big worry.

Most of the time, we were just looking to get somewhere to play more hockey. We'd play every day after school, and on the weekends we'd go from early morning until late at night. Imagine a game that lasted for twelve hours with kids coming and going. I'd play for hours, then when I got cold or hungry I'd skate back home. It's been said that, while growing up, I ate meals with my skates on. It's true. Mum would spread newspapers over the linoleum floor in our house, so my brothers and friends and I could come inside on our skates. After we warmed up and had something to eat, we'd head right back outside. It was as if we hadn't left the game. We'd just ask someone the score and start playing again.

Anyone who's ever gone to a rink and stepped onto a sheet of freshly Zambonied ice knows it's something special. It's so smooth and perfect, it's like a canvas. And that's what you get just at a local arena. Move up to the NHL and skating onto a fresh sheet of ice is like being in a cathedral. Playing outside is something different altogether. The ice isn't pristine like it is indoors. It'll be uneven in spots and have ripples and ridges and bumps in others. I've always been strong on my skates, and I give some of the credit to spending my childhood skating outside on different kinds of ice in all types of conditions. Once I got to proper rinks, the ice was so nice it was like cheating. It really let you fly.

Nowadays it seems that kids don't play much hockey unless it's organized. I understand that times have changed, but I always figured that the way to get better at something is to do it as much as possible. Maybe I was too single-minded at times, but that's the way I was with hockey.

A number of years ago I remember asking some young guys if they ever played hockey with a tennis ball. They said it was pucks for them, mostly. I think that's a shame. When I was a kid we would play ball hockey on the road or in driveways all the time. With a tennis ball, you're basically playing with a bouncing puck. You can't force a tennis ball; you need to be light of hand to control it, so playing with one really helps to develop your touch. Plus, if you play it against a wall, when it comes back your way either you learn how to trap it with your stick blade or you end up spending your time chasing it down the street. I didn't like chasing tennis balls too much, so I became pretty good at trapping them out of the air. I told these youngsters that was how I practiced as a kid. Whenever I went anywhere, I was stickhandling a ball down the road.

Years later I read a story about Steve Nash, the basketball player. When he was in college, he used to dribble a tennis ball around campus on his way to class. He won a couple of MVP awards in the NBA, so I guess a tennis ball helped him out, too.

Growing up, I would spend hours shooting a ball or a puck at the side of our house. We had a shingled veranda, which ran about two-thirds of the way around the house. It made a great target. I'd sit back and fire away, breaking more than a few of the shingles in the process. After a while, the veranda started to get down to the bare planks. One day, my dad came out of the house, took a look at it, and shook his head at me. He didn't get too angry, though. Instead, he took me for a walk down to the Quaker Oats mill. We found a couple of big plywood sheets that had come off the railroad grain cars and Dad carried them home. He leaned one up against the house, put the other down on the driveway, and told me to keep shooting as much as I wanted.

Over the years, some folks have suggested that my father was too hard on me. He was stern, sure. And he was tough. He also had to work a lot to keep food on the table, so he wasn't around for the kids like Mum was, but that doesn't mean he didn't care. The Depression made for tough times everywhere, but the Prairies were hit particularly hard. Wheat was the major crop, and when the bottom fell out of the market, it took Saskatchewan down with it. Not that farmers were able to grow much during a drought anyway, maybe a couple of bushels an acre if they were fortunate. The summers then were hotter and drier than any I've seen since, and when the wind came up there was nothing to stop the topsoil from blowing away. It was called the Dirty Thirties for a reason. Even as a kid, I understood that Saskatoon was in bad shape. There was hardly any work and there wasn't anything going on. I remember feeling lucky that my dad had a job. I knew other families that were on relief; that's what social assistance was called at the time. Dad couldn't be involved in my life the way parents are these days, but he was still there for us in a way that fathers were back then.

One lesson he taught me that stuck with me throughout my hockey career was not to take any dirt from anyone, because if you do they'll just keep giving it to you. He wouldn't take any dirt and he told me not to either. When I was a bit older we were playing pool one night at a tavern, and this guy kept bumping Dad's hand when he was about to shoot. Dad gave the guy a warning, but the guy wouldn't stop. Why this guy wanted to get my father going, I don't know. One thing he should have known: My dad never hit with his fists in case he broke a knuckle. He used the heel of his hand instead. So this guy kept trying to get into it with Dad, bumping his pool cue, until Dad finally stepped back and drilled him. My father was a powerful man and the guy's whole body cleared the end of the table. The owner came over and said, "Ab, you better get out of here. I think you killed him." The punch put the guy down for the count, but he turned out to be more or less okay. I'll bet his manners around a pool table improved afterward as well. That was Dad. Don't take any dirt from anybody.

When I played hockey and I'd go into the corner after a puck, my dad's lesson was probably somewhere in the back of my head. Don't take any dirt from this guy or it'll keep coming all game long. I like to think some guys weren't too keen to give me anything extra along the boards because they knew I wouldn't be shy about giving it right back.

The first time I realized I might be pretty strong I was maybe eight years old. I was on a teeter-totter with my brother Vic and an older kid pushed him off. Well, I was on the other end and slammed down pretty hard. My butt hurt when I got off the ground and I wasn't too happy about it. I never liked bullies so I packed up a snowball with some cinders, reared back, and fired it at the kid's head. It caught him square in the side of the face and they had to dig cinders out of his eye for about an hour. It didn't end up doing too much damage, just a bit of irritation and he had to wear an eye patch for a while.

As you might expect, he didn't take too kindly to what happened. He came to square things up not long after and found me in the school washroom. He was in the eighth grade and a pretty big guy. I had good size for my age, but I was only in the third grade. I remember thinking that the kid looked as big as my dad and I'd be lucky to get out of there with my life. He hauled off and swung at me, trying to hit me in the head, but I jumped and the punch caught me in the chest instead. It didn't really hurt. Maybe it was the adrenaline I had going, but I remember not feeling it at all. I swung back instinctively and wound up hitting him in the same eye that I'd nailed with the snowball. His hands went to his face and that fight was over. I don't know if I was tough or not, but nobody really bothered me from then on, so I guess it worked out as well as it could have.

Growing up, I probably raised a bit more hell than I should have. I like to think I was a pretty good kid, but sometimes things just seemed like a good idea even though they probably weren't. I remember once when I was in about second grade we made our own golf course near our house. We cut the grass as best we could, put a little sand on it to make it smooth, and that was our first hole. So we were out there playing some golf and having a great time, but there was a family that lived nearby that was pretty miserable. As far as they were concerned, nobody should ever have any fun. We were playing and suddenly the police showed up and told us we had to stop. The couple had called the cops on us. And this wasn't the only time. Anything we did, even just playing ball, they'd tell us we couldn't do it. We didn't think we were bothering anybody so we didn't think too much of them.

Some time later I was walking along and saw someone burning some old tires. Boy, did it kick up a vicious smoke. Well, I got to thinking about that and one day we decided to get a bunch of old tires together. We piled them up not far from that neighbor's house and waited for the wind to blow just right. We had scrounged some gasoline and we poured it on the tires and lit the pile. So this thick, black smoke started billowing up and it blew straight into their house. They came running out, trying to put out the fire, but they couldn't. We stayed out of sight and watched. I'm sure they suspected us, but nobody ever came knocking on our door. I guess you could say we were mean little buggers, but it felt like maybe they had it coming.

We did some rough things, I suppose. One day, we were out near a golf course looking for stray balls, which we used to sell back to the golfers, and we started getting cold. We figured we'd warm ourselves with a little fire. One of the kids gathered up a bunch of dry grass and we lit it. Well, the fire started going like crazy and suddenly we had a thirty-foot wall of flames. We tried putting it out, but there was just no way. So we ran like hell, went over to the railroad station, pulled the alarm, and kept right on going.

The one thing I did that maybe bothered me the most came a few years later. In those days, none of us could really afford anything. One day a bunch of us figured we wanted to have a big corn roast, but we didn't have any good supplies so we decided we'd try to get some. We went out back of Livergant's store and staged a fight. I was one of the fighters and we had a bunch of guys make a big racket, cheering us on. We were out there going at it like crazy, pretending we were serious, until the folks inside got curious enough to come out and check on the commotion. When that happened, a guy ran into the store and stole a pound of butter. Afterward, we went out to a cornfield, helped ourselves to a few heads of corn, and boiled 'em up over a fire. Borrowing from farmers was pretty common. Sometimes it was corn, other times it was carrots or potatoes. So we were having this corn roast and it was delicious because we had the butter, but something about it didn't quite sit right with me.

I knew another fellow, a pretty good hockey player actually, who needed a shoelace once. He didn't have the money for it, so he took a wire hanger, straightened it out, and made a little hook on the end. Then he went into a store and tried to lift a lace off the wall using the hook. Well, he got caught. That little lace kept him out of the United States, because when he applied for a green card eventually, the theft was on his record. He couldn't go anywhere. Knowing what happened to him put a pretty good scare into me. The deal with the butter, I can tell you, was the beginning and the end of my career as a juvenile delinquent.

Most of the time we weren't getting into much trouble, though, just running around looking to play whatever sport was in season. I had a big group of friends and we did everything together. We'd go from hockey to football to soccer and then to baseball. We loved getting on the ball diamond in the summertime. And we played some pretty good baseball in Saskatchewan. At the start of my career in Detroit I was still going back to Saskatoon to play semi-pro ball in the summers. That stopped in about 1952, when Jack Adams, the team's general manager, became too worried that I might get hurt. That wasn't ever a thought when we were little.

Playing sports was a pretty big deal to all of us. It might have meant even more to me than most. I was a shy kid and I can't say I was a great student. Kids were pretty rough on me around school. Sometimes they called me "Doughhead," which wouldn't make any kid feel great. I ended up failing third grade and that really hurt. I was pretty broken up over it. I went to summer school and devoted a lot of time to learning something there. I knew I wasn't lazy, but I always had a tough time with spelling. It comes easy to some people, but words always gave me some trouble. I was better with numbers. I never really talked to people too much about it, though. Years later, my son Marty was diagnosed with dyslexia when he was just little. It's occurred to me that I might have something like that myself.

As an adult, I've done crossword puzzles my whole life to help me with my spelling and vocabulary. They're also a great way to kill time when you're traveling to away games. I've actually come across my own name in crosswords a number of times. It's quite a thrill. I've seen Bobby Orr's name as well—and it's even easier to spell.

Any problems I might have had in the classroom seemed to go away when I was playing sports, especially hockey. I was able to pick up skills quickly, and I found that once I was on the ice I could outplay the kids who teased me when we were off it. Hockey became sort of a sanctuary, I guess. You didn't have to talk too much; you could just play. Any time I could play, I would.

One day I was skating on the sloughs with a friend, Frank Shedden. We'd skate along, walk over the roads, and skate some more. Sometimes the water in the sloughs would be four or five feet deep. If you felt the ice start to give a bit, you'd have to skate like crazy to make sure you didn't break through. I was ahead of Frank and we could feel the ice start to soften, so we were skating hard until suddenly I heard a crack and a splash. I turned around and saw that Frank had fallen through the ice. The water had even gone over his head for a second. I pulled him out eventually, but we had about a mile to go to get him home. It was freezing cold that day and we were both scared for him. Have you ever seen a clothesline in a high wind with a pair of long johns flying on it as stiff as a board? That was how Frank looked when we staggered into his house. He got awfully sick after that, probably with pneumonia.

The next day I went over to see how Frank was doing. Things weren't good. His dad said he'd be out of commission for a while. Mr. Shedden was a really nice man. He asked me if I was trying out for the Peewee hockey team. I was about eleven years old, and although I played on outdoor rinks and ponds all the time,

I'd never played in a real game of organized hockey. To do that you needed proper equipment, and my family just didn't have the money. I told Mr. Shedden that I wasn't trying out because I didn't have the right gear. He went into the house, rounded up all of Frank's equipment, and handed it over. Frank would be laid up for a few months, he said, so I might as well make use of the equipment to try out. Well, I ended up making that team and Mr. Shedden let me keep some of Frank's things. His skates had nickel-plated blades. I'd never worn skates so nice in my life. They were beautiful. I could really fly with those blades. Half the time I was on the ice, I just wanted to look down to admire them. I'm sure Mr. Shedden never understood exactly what he did for me that day, but I've never forgotten it.

As I look back on growing up, one thing I know for certain is that nobody ever makes it anywhere on their own. I was lucky enough to have folks like Mr. Shedden looking out for me along the way. I'm very grateful for that. And he's not the only person I wish a young Gordie Howe could go back and thank.

I'd guess that every hockey fan (and probably almost every Canadian) knows the story of how Wayne Gretzky learned the game as a boy on the backyard rink that his dad built. My family didn't have a rink, but a number of families in Saskatoon, like the Hodges, did at the time.

The Hodges had two sons who played hockey and they kept a nearly full-sized rink in their backyard. They didn't mind too much who was over there playing or when, as long as you were respectful. I spent a lot of time there. Sometimes we'd play shinny and other times it would just be me. I'd go over in the morning and if it had snowed overnight I'd shovel the rink off and skate before school. I'd make up drills for myself and go around and around the rink stickhandling and shooting. At night, I'd stay there until after it got dark. It would be freezing on some nights, but for some reason I never really felt the cold that much when I was playing.

Equipment was always a big problem for us as kids. We'd hang around the rink and scrounge some of the beaten-up stuff that older players threw away. I'd find old shin pads that were just like a few bamboo poles, all ripped up with pieces missing, but I didn't care. I'd wrap them around my legs and put rubber bands around my pants to hold it all together. Sometimes I'd make homemade shin guards out of magazines. I'd even use stuff that other rink rats had found, used, and thrown away again. I'd take it home, sew the heck out of the gloves or whatever else, and use it until it fell apart. I remember that my mother, who gave our neighbor a few dollars for my first pair of skates, also got me my second pair. A man brought them to the door and she traded him a pack of my father's cigarettes for them. I'm not sure how Dad felt about that. I know I never asked.

We treasured our sticks, as well. We'd do anything to keep them usable. We'd use glue, tape, tack a little metal onto them, whatever we could do to keep them together. Eventually, though, they'd wear down from playing in the street. You'd be playing with a toothpick, just hoping it would make it through the day. When it finally went for good, it would break your heart.

There wasn't much money to go around during the Depression, but folks still looked out for local kids. I remember a fellow by the name of Roly Howes. He owned a hardware store and he was pretty good to me. His store sold sporting goods and one day Mum took me there to buy me a hockey stick for my birthday. He knew my team was in the playoffs against another town, and he told me that if I scored a hat trick in the next game, he'd give me a pair of hockey gloves. We used to count the number of rolls on the back of the gloves to determine how nice they were. Cheap gloves didn't have any rolls; they were just one solid piece. Five rolls was the ultimate.

Mr. Howes knew how we dressed. He saw us playing in regular street pants with pads underneath held on by rubber bands, so he knew how much equipment meant to us. The playoff game came around and I ended up getting 12 points: 4 goals and 8 assists. I went back to the store and Mr. Howes told me that since I'd exceeded the hat trick, he'd decided to throw in a pair of shin pads as well. The gloves he gave me had four rolls on them. I loved those gloves.

I owe a lot to folks like that growing up. My sisters were also really good to me. We grew up together in an old house that was heated with wood and coal. You always kept your socks on at night, because when the fire went out the house would get cold. There was frost everywhere by morning. Dad used to staple plastic around the windows or stuff felt along the inside of the window edges to try to keep the cold out. We didn't have indoor plumbing and we used to take a lot of our baths at school. Still, my sisters and my mum found a way to keep me in hockey equipment and make sure I could travel to games. They'd come and cheer, too. When you're a kid, I don't know if you appreciate everything that people do for you, but looking back on those days, that's what I think about. I spent a lot of time on the ice practicing, and I worked hard, but it would be wrong to think that I got to the NHL on my own.

My memories are filled with people who went out of their way to help me, when the most they could possibly have expected in return was a thank-you. All these years later, I'm still grateful.

Growing up during the Depression we didn't have much, but we had each other, we had our friends, and that was pretty much all we needed. I was aware that some people had more, but those who did, shared. Folks shared a lot back then. It was a different time. People cared about their neighbors and looked out for one another. If somebody needed help, they got it, and if you could give it, you did.

Kids today probably can't imagine what it's like to grow up with so little, but I don't think about it as not having had a lot of stuff. We had everything we needed. I look back on my childhood and I feel lucky.

*Two*

# GROWING UP IN SASKATOON

My dad bought our first radio when I was six or seven. Before it arrived in our house we used to go over to a friend's to listen to our favorite shows. When we got our own, it became something like the family hearth. We spent hours staring at that radio, and I can still picture it clearly. It was only about eighteen inches tall, brown wood, rounded at the top with three small knobs at the bottom. It was just a little box, but it opened up our whole world.

I can still hear Foster Hewitt's voice coming into our home on a Saturday night. We'd tune in to hear him say, "Hello, Canada, and hockey fans in the United States and Newfoundland," and it was as if we were rinkside at a game thousands of miles away. As an announcer, Hewitt was so talented that we didn't need a television to picture what was happening on the ice. He made the game come alive in your imagination.

Back then, it seemed like everyone listened to hockey games on the radio. As I got older, when Hewitt would deliver his trademark "He shoots, he scores!" I'd imagine he was calling a goal scored by Gordie Howe. Kids all over the country probably had the same dream. Sometimes I shake my head at the fact that mine actually came true.

One of the most satisfying things about getting an NHL paycheck was having the wherewithal to make things easier for Mum. When we were growing up, she didn't have any of the things that most of us now can't imagine living without. No plumbing. No iron. No range. Not that it occurred to anyone—and certainly not to my mother—to complain. She was such a soft-spoken, thoughtful woman, yet tough at the same time. She never complained about a thing. I don't think it ever occurred to her that she had it hard, despite the fact that she spent hours doing chores that would take only a few minutes today.

When my brother Vern went away to serve in World War II, his wife, Amelia, moved in with us. I remember sitting with her and going through Eaton's catalogs, picking out different things I would buy for Mum when I made it to the big leagues. For someone who was barely a teenager, I could really run up a bill providing her with washing machines and refrigerators. I think it's one explanation for why I practiced as hard as I did. The main reason was always just love of the game, but as I got older the idea of playing professional hockey started to become less of a childhood fantasy and more of a real possibility.

By the time I was ten or eleven I was playing as much organized hockey as I could. I think that five was the most teams I ever played for at one time. I attended King George School and played on our school team. Then there was a mercantile league that local businesspeople put together. I played with my local Peewee team and then Bantam hockey as I got older. I played on a church team and also on one for pick-up games. I'd just change sweaters and go from one game to the next. For a kid who loved to play, it didn't get any better than that.

Playing sports now seems so much more specialized. Everything is structured. If you play hockey, that doesn't leave much time for anything else. Hockey was definitely my sport of choice, but I played whatever sport was in season. Athletically, I think it was good for me. The balance, speed, strength, and agility I developed playing different sports all contributed to what I could do on the ice. These days they call it cross-training, or at least they used to. There might be another name for it now. When we were kids, we just called it playing.

Most hockey fans, if they think about it, probably see me coming down the right wing. That's where I played in Detroit, but it didn't start out that way. Way back when, I actually began playing in net. In fact, I was in net for the first truly big game I ever played.

I was around thirteen at the time and I was between the pipes for our school team, King George, which won the championship. The way things worked back then, two players from each school were selected to play in an all-star game. It was a big honor to be chosen and I was proud to represent our school. The game pitted Saskatoon's East and West school districts against each other and it seemed like everyone in the city had a rooting interest. The rink held about four thousand people and it was packed—standing room only. The men, of course, all wore hats and the women wore gloves. In those days, when you went for an evening out, you dressed for it.

I remember the crowd well, because I had a great view from the bench. As happy as I was to make the team, I was pretty disappointed that a goalie from a different school was picked to start. When the puck dropped, there I was on the bench, excited to be there but unable to do much to help my team. As it turned out, things didn't go so well for the first-stringer. The other team scored 3 goals in about the first five minutes. We were already nervous playing in front of such a big crowd and suddenly we were down by 3 quick goals. Our coach gave the goalie the hook, and in I went. The boys showed a lot of heart that night. We steadied the ship and won the game by a final score of 6–4.

The coach of my school team at King George, Mr. Trickey, was also our vice principal. Not only was he my coach but also he was a big part of the reason I finally started to enjoy school. He really took an interest in me as a student. We'd go over problems and he'd help me out with whatever I needed. It's amazing what a good teacher can do for a kid. As good as he was to me, though, he did get one thing pretty wrong.

When I was playing goal for King George, I'd ask Mr. Trickey if I could play out sometimes, rather than stay in net. His answer? He thought it was in everyone's best interests for me to stay in net. In fact, he told me that playing goalie would be the only way I'd get out of Saskatoon as a hockey player. We both ended up being happy that he was wrong. For some twenty years after I made it to the NHL, I'd send him letters to remind him of that. We actually became pretty close friends as adults and always made a point of getting together when I came back to town.

I don't think anybody achieves much without the Robert Trickeys of the world. Growing up, we were lucky that Saskatoon was full of good people who spent a lot of time looking out for the local kids. I played in all sorts of leagues and they all had coaches, referees, and other volunteers who made it possible for kids to play organized sports. At the King George Athletic Club I couldn't guess how many kids benefited from the hard work of people like Buck and Doris Crawford and Bert and Frances Hodges. As it turned out, quite a few of us made it from Saskatchewan to the NHL. It wouldn't have happened without folks like them, but there was more to it than just getting a few players to the big leagues. They made the lives of a lot of kids, including me, just a bit better. To me, that feels like something special.

The community looked out for us in ways both big and small. There was a system in Saskatoon to make sure we deserved our ice time. We didn't just show up at the rink to play. You had to prove that you had been behaving yourself, by collecting signatures from people who would attest to the fact that you hadn't been up to mischief. Before you could get on the ice, you needed to get your permission paper signed by a parent, one of your teachers, and someone from the church. I guess it was a way to instill some discipline in us and make sure we toed the line. If getting into trouble meant you couldn't play, you were pretty likely to keep your nose clean.

Naturally, we still knew ways to work the system. Sometimes we'd go to services at the Salvation Army hall and get the people there to sign, which counted as a church signature. They were pretty good to us. In the middle of a service they'd even stop to announce that there were four young men who were due on the ice very shortly. We'd get up, smile thankfully at the people who were letting us out of the pews, and hustle our way down to the rink.

As it turned out, being a goalie did more for me as a hockey player than I could have realized. Over my career I was fortunate enough to put the puck in the net more than my fair share. One of the skills that helped me score some of those goals was the ability to shoot the puck with both hands. You don't see that much anymore.

I've heard people say that I'm naturally ambidextrous, but that's not exactly true.

The reason I could shoot from both the right side and the left side goes back to playing goalie as a kid. As you can imagine, proper goaltender equipment was expensive and pretty tough to come by. When I was scuffling around for gear, the only thing I could find for a catching glove was a first-baseman's mitt that went on my left hand. If I was a left-handed shot that would have been fine, but I shot right—and there is no way you can shoot right with a catcher's mitt on your left hand. Since the glove was dictating the terms, I didn't have much choice. I learned to shoot the puck as a goalie, clearing it up the ice and steering it into the corners, from the left side. When I played out as a defenseman or forward, I would flip back to shooting from the right side. That's how I developed a shot from both sides, but for a long time I didn't realize I was switching hands. I just shot whichever way I thought had the best chance of putting the puck in the net.

It wasn't until my first training camp with the Red Wings, when I was sixteen, that I found out I was doing something out of the ordinary. I went in on one of the goalies during a practice, switched hands, and scored. Jack Adams, the coach at the time, was watching. He called me over with a gruff "What are you doing?"

"What's that, sir?" I asked.

He stuck his chin out toward the goalie and said, "You shoot both ways."

I hadn't ever thought about it, so I asked, "I do?" I had no idea. After growing up playing every position on the ice, it just seemed natural.

My early experience in net helped my career in other ways, as well. Spending time between the pipes didn't just teach me how to shoot the puck. It taught me *where* to shoot it. When you're in net you see the ice—and more importantly the puck—from an entirely different perspective than you do as a skater. I used to think of the puck as having eyes. What it sees is totally different than what you see as a shooter. When you're coming in on net, the goalie doesn't see you as much as you might think he does. What he sees is the puck. Since the goalie is focused on the puck, as a shooter it only makes sense to think about things from the puck's point of view. I envisioned the net and the goaltender from the puck's perspective on the ice, instead of from what my eyes saw six feet higher up. I didn't have to beat the goalie after all. That's the puck's job. Knowing what I saw as a goalie helped me understand where the puck needed to be to score. Any player who's ever suffered through a cold spell knows that when you're in a slump, all you see is the goalie. His pads and blocker seem to take up the whole net. But when you're hot, it's like he's not even there. All you see is the mesh behind him. I visualized the puck seeing those empty spaces around the goalie and finding itself in the back of the net.

In any case, as much as I liked playing goalie, I'm glad I never had to go between the pipes in the NHL, particularly back when I started and goalies didn't wear masks. As a kid, sometimes I'd stand under a lamppost at night and let the guys on the team take shots at me to practice. I didn't have a mask or a jock at the time. That meant I had to be fast, *very* fast, especially on shots below the waist.

We were lucky to play as much hockey as we did, but we certainly did more than just play sports. As far back as I can recall, my brothers and sisters and I were always working at something, whether it was chores or part-time jobs when we weren't in school.

We didn't have running water; no one in our neighborhood did. The streets in Saskatoon are laid out according to the alphabet, and in those days, streets from L Street down weren't serviced by a water main, and that included us. The city kept a tap on every other block, and it was up to each household to carry water home from there. We had a forty-five-gallon drum at our house to store water. In summer it sat outside on the porch, and in the winter we moved it inside to keep the water from freezing. Winter or summer, though, that drum always seemed to need filling. And that job fell to the kids.

The trouble was, there was no way we could lift a full drum, never mind carry it. At best, we could maybe fill it halfway before we packed it back to the house. To top it up, there was no way around it: We had to haul pails of water. It was uphill-going for about half a city block. We were also on sandy soil, so your feet would sink a little. Trudging back from that tap with those heavy pails wasn't fun, but it actually turned out to be pretty good training for my legs. I've often thought that lugging those pails made me stronger on my skates.

Having to carry water uphill made it something too precious to see wasted, and I kept a close eye on that drum. Occasionally Dad would dip a pail in to water the garden. We had an acre in the backyard that we planted every year. The vegetables we grew meant a lot to the family. What we didn't eat, we'd end up taking door-to-door to sell. Still, seeing water from that drum get dumped on the ground drove me crazy.

I did odd jobs for as long as I can remember. When I was eight years old, I started delivering pamphlets for Livergant's, a local grocery store. My area was about six square blocks. There were no mailboxes on the street, so the pamphlet either slid through a slit in the front door or you knocked and handed it to someone in person. In the winter, I often chose the personal touch. When it's thirty below, you hope a kind neighbor will invite you in to warm up. Delivering those flyers earned me thirty-five cents a day. Even as a kid I was big enough to handle the store's bicycle, so in the summer I'd deliver groceries for Livergant's. The sandy soil made for some tough riding, but I made better money doing that than I did with the pamphlets.

We also used to earn money by hunting gophers. Those who live in a city nowadays might think that sounds inhumane, but if you live in the country you know that gophers are no friend to farmers and ranchers. They eat crops and dig holes that can trip up a cow or a horse. As an animal lover, I don't look back on my gopher-killing days with much joy, but it was a good way for a kid to earn some money. Much of the time we'd get them with homemade slingshots. We used to be paid one cent a tail. It might not sound like much, but every penny counted. We'd gather up our tails, sometimes more than a hundred, and walk to a spot about ten miles out of town to collect our money.

Sometimes we'd splurge with that money. Going to the movies cost a nickel and our gopher earnings would buy us popcorn and maybe candy as well. On some occasions we were less than honest about getting into the theater. One of us would buy a ticket, then head to the back door and sneak the rest of us inside. It seems unscrupulous in hindsight, but when you grow up in a family with nine kids and very little money to go around you learn how to cut some corners to get by.

Another way I earned money that didn't seem like work at all was by fishing. I've loved to fish my whole life. When I was about eleven I saved up my money and bought a fishing pole with a reel on it. Even then, I think I was a decent little fisherman. I'd catch ten or twenty fish a day and run them over to a Chinese restaurant in town. I'd bang on the back door and sell them for five or ten cents each. It was a good arrangement for both of us. Years later, after Colleen and I were married, we were visiting Saskatoon and she asked to see that restaurant. We drove over and went in and sat down. I felt like a kid again when I realized that the original owner was still there. He didn't recognize me, though. That is, he knew me as Gordie Howe of the Detroit Red Wings but he was stunned when I told him I was the little guy who used to sell him fish. I gave him a hard time and let him know he should have paid me more. He thought I was kidding, but I'm still not entirely sure if I was. We had a good laugh about it, though, and I was glad that Colleen and I got to share a small part of my childhood.

Anyone who marries a fisherman, like Colleen did, can tell you that sometimes it will be your privilege to hear a good fish story. She was lucky enough to listen to this one a few times. When I was just a kid, I once caught an eleven-pound pike when all I had was a little cane pole. I was fishing near a guy who spotted a pike in the water, pointed at it, and told me to throw in a line to see if I could catch it. My hook was baited with a piece of beef heart, so I cast it over and the pike hit it straightaway. I yanked the pole up, but the fish was so big it broke the rod. I grabbed at the string and, even though the line bit into my hands, managed to wrestle the pike in close enough to stab it with my knife. It was a hell of a fight for a little guy like me. I was so excited to land that fish I jumped on my bike and took it to show my dad at work. He brought it home, chopped it up, and that pike fed the family for a while.

Another job I enjoyed as a kid was caddying at the local golf course. I loved to golf and I loved being on a golf course. I still do, in fact. Even at twelve or thirteen years old I could get around a course fairly well. A lot of hockey players I know are naturals with a golf club in their hands. The mechanics of shooting a puck and swinging a golf club aren't exactly the same, but they do have similarities. It helps to be good with your hands, for one thing. In both cases, the amount of lag you create as your hands pass through the contact zone helps to generate power.

I've been lucky in my life to be able to make money by fishing, golfing, and playing hockey. To be fair, I earned a bit more from hockey than the other two, but a paycheck is still a paycheck.

When I got older, the work I did became more physical, but that was partly by choice. I'd noticed that the best players on the ice always seemed to be the strongest guys, and that's who I wanted to be. I was always preparing for the next hockey season and I tried to pick jobs that would help with that. Since I was big for my age, my father was usually able to put me to work doing something. Much of the time it was just moving heavy stuff from one pile to another. Dad did a lot of concrete work, which meant there were always cement bags to carry. My dad had the type of strength you get only by working with your hands for a lifetime. He used to lift things I wouldn't even attempt. Watching him made me want to work harder. I would pick up bags of cement that weighed about ninety pounds apiece, one in each hand, and haul them to the mixer. The weight wasn't the toughest thing to manage; it was the sacks themselves. They were packed so tightly there was no place to grip them. I would grit my teeth, clamp down on them, and pick them up. I figured the payoff for building up my hand strength would come when the season started. On top of that, Dad was always bragging to the other guys about how much his kid could lift, so I never wanted to embarrass him by dropping a bag.

Working manual labor after school and on weekends became routine when I was about fourteen. I was big enough to do it and the pay was definitely appreciated. I could run a cement mixer, which earned a mechanic's wage of around eighty cents an hour. Regular workers made fifty cents an hour. I kept my head down and worked hard to make sure the older men wouldn't resent a young guy earning a higher wage. I remember that old cement mixer took forty-two shovels of gravel for every load. After filling the drum, you'd add powdered cement and then keep water running into it constantly as it mixed. Years later, I was watching television and saw *The Karate Kid*. In the movie the old sensei, Mr. Miyagi, trains his pupil using household chores. It occurred to me that waxing a car and painting a fence would have been a lot easier than carrying cement bags and shoveling gravel. In the end, though, I got stronger and the kid won the karate tournament, so I guess both approaches did the trick.

One guy my dad used to work with was named Frenchy. He lived nearby with his wife and kids. He was always good to me, so I went to Dad one day and asked if he'd switch my paycheck with Frenchy's. I was making the extra wages as a mechanic and I knew the money would mean more to someone who had a whole family to feed. It was a small gesture, but it felt like the right thing to do. Frenchy ended up telling the other guys on the crew about it, which wasn't the point, but it did smooth things out at work. After that the older men thought I was all right, which was fine by me. I kept on with the job, which was basically the equivalent of doing a daily weight-training program without even knowing it. By fifteen years old, I was six feet tall and around two hundred pounds. I was a big kid, but I figured I'd end up huge if I kept growing. I leveled off right around there, so it didn't turn out that way. I played my whole career at six feet tall and usually between 196 and 204 pounds, pretty much the same size I was as a teenager.

For a young hockey player, getting on the ice with older players is always a thrill. My sons Mark and Marty did it when they were young, and so did I. Being among the better players on the ice isn't always a good thing for young players. When you skate with full-grown men, it can be an eye-opener. The game changes. Everything is faster, so you have to do everything faster—skate, pass, think—to keep up. When you go back to playing with your own age group, the game slows down. When that happens for you in any sport, it's a beautiful thing.

During the war, the senior club in Saskatoon would occasionally run a few players short, so they'd ask some younger guys to fill in. One night when I was around fourteen or so, we played in a town with a crowd that really hated the boys from Saskatoon. In the pre-television era, and even long after, senior hockey was the biggest game in town. And it was good hockey. Before the national hockey program began, it was the top senior club in the country that represented Canada internationally. Back then, the best senior team in Canada was arguably the best team in the world.

In any case, people took it very seriously, and when we started taking it to the home team that night, the fans turned on us. They were throwing things and spitting at us. When the home team realized that they couldn't skate with us, they decided to show a little muscle. A fight led to a line brawl, and soon the benches cleared. Not wanting to be left out, some of the fans decided to join in and hopped over the boards to mix it up. I'd never seen anything like it. One of the veterans on our team put me behind him and told me to watch his back. If anyone rushed up on us, he told me to smack them on the head with my stick.

I was pretty scared, so I listened to those instructions very carefully. The scene on the ice was crazy. I was trying to keep an eye on all of the fights around me when I saw someone coming up on us at a run. I knew what I was supposed to do, and I didn't hesitate. I raised my stick and cracked him on the head. Down he went. As he crumpled on the ice, I looked down and noticed something I hadn't a moment earlier: a yellow stripe on his pants. In Canada, that means only one thing. He wasn't a player. He wasn't a referee. He wasn't even a fan. He was RCMP, a member of the Royal Canadian Mounted Police. I had just clubbed a Mountie. I wish he had identified himself before charging at me. It would have saved me a lot of worrying, and him a lump on his head. My teammate grabbed me and we got out of there. I was sure they'd come after me for that and I'd land in jail, but days passed and thankfully no one knocked on our door.

I guess maybe that Mountie didn't catch my number, so he didn't know who to come find. In my hockey career I never had much trouble knowing who did right by me and who had earned some payback. I definitely took numbers. Another night that stands out for me growing up was a game we played against the Bentley brothers, Max and Doug. They were from Delisle, Saskatchewan, and three of the Bentley brothers were playing in the NHL that season. I was only about fourteen and it was one of those games where I could have skated forever. I was young and fresh and excited to be skating against big-time players. I had a ton of jump in my legs that night and I scored a few goals early. We had them down 4–0 and I was flying along the wing when suddenly Doug Bentley, who played for the Black Hawks, speared me in the belly. I doubled over onto the ice in agony. I was down there sucking wind when Max, who was about eight years older than me, looked down and said, "Slow down, damn you." Part of me took it as a compliment. But only part. The next time I played against Doug was years later in the NHL. He was still with Chicago and I was with Detroit. Only this time, the shoe was on the other foot. He was coming down the wing, clearly having no recollection of the object lesson he'd delivered so many years ago in Saskatchewan, when I drilled him. Now it was my turn to offer some advice to a guy crumpled on the ice. I leaned over and said, "Slow down, damn you." I figured we were even after that. I might have carried a grudge, but once a score was settled, I was willing to move on. Over the years, I ended up playing baseball with quite a few of the Bentley brothers. They were good guys and great athletes.

Around that same time, I got the chance to skate against another NHL player, Harry Watson. He was from Saskatoon and started in the league around 1940. When the war escalated, he interrupted his hockey career to join the Canadian military, ending up back in Saskatoon at the Royal Canadian Air Force Station. The base was a pretty big deal at that time, with pilots and air crews coming in from all over the Commonwealth to be trained by the British and Canadian militaries. When you fly into Saskatoon today, the airport is on the same spot as the old RCAF landing strip. While in the service, Watson kept up his hockey skills by playing for the squad run by the No. 4 Service Flying Training School. I played against them one night and after the game Watson sought me out to find out my name. I was flattered that he thought I played well enough to ask. About four years later

I was in my first season with the Red Wings when I found myself going up against none other than Harry Watson, who was playing left wing for Toronto. Early in the game I turned to chase a puck into the corner, and he was right on my shoulder. He could have put a big hit on me, but instead he slowed down and gave me a warning I never forgot, "Look out, Gordie!" It was a rough league back then, so that was pretty rare. After the play moved on I gave him a look, but didn't say anything.

A period or two later we were heading into the corner again, only this time it was his head that was down. I can remember a good deed just as well as a liberty taken that needs retribution. "Look out, Mr. Watson!" I yelled. He slowed up and we froze the puck with our skates until the whistle blew. He looked over at me and said, "We're gonna get along just fine." We were both Saskatchewan boys, so that might have counted for something, or maybe he was just a class act, but for whatever reason, we extended that courtesy to each other for the rest of our careers. It goes without saying that you always play to win, but that doesn't mean you need to scrape every inch out of every play, regardless of whether it puts another player at risk. When I watch sports these days, I don't always see players respect their opponents the way they should. It's a tough game, and I wouldn't have gotten very far if I hadn't been willing to lean on a guy from time to time. And sometimes you're going to have to take a hit to make a play. But that doesn't mean you waive your right to be treated with respect.

In my younger days, my hero was Ab Welsh. He was a great player and, like Harry Watson, he carried himself with a lot of class. In 1934, he was a member of the Saskatoon Quakers, the city's senior team that went overseas to Italy and won a gold medal for Canada at the World Championships. As a kid, I would hang around the rink all the time, looking for ways to get in. I'd wait outside and when the refreshments arrived for the players, I'd volunteer to help deliver them to the dressing rooms. Other times, I'd wait until the bus pulled up and ask if any equipment needed to be carried. The players knew how much watching a game meant to us, and they treated the local kids pretty well. Maybe they remembered being young players themselves. When I made the big leagues, I know I tried not to forget how I'd felt as a kid. One time, Ab Welsh brought me into the dressing room and I collected an autograph from every player. Then he asked which way I shot. I told him right. He said "good" and handed me a stick. I couldn't believe it. It was about the first new stick I'd ever had. That kind gesture meant a heck of a lot to me. I walked out of there floating. It was a beautiful stick. Ab Welsh didn't know it, but he made a friend for life that day. That stick actually ended up having a big influence on my career. It was a lie seven, which refers to the angle of the blade compared to the shaft. I ended up using that same lie for the rest of my career.

Growing up, I had a lot of good hockey role models. Not only did I have local players like Ab Welsh to admire, but we also had Foster Hewitt to describe the players in the NHL. Television wasn't around yet, but we still knew what players looked like, which helped our imagination when listening to the radio. The credit for that belonged to BeeHive Corn Syrup. You may wonder what corn syrup has to do with hockey. I'll bet nearly every Canadian kid who grew up around that time could tell you the answer. If you sent a BeeHive Corn Syrup label to the company, they'd send back a picture of the hockey player of your choice. The photo was black and white and a decent size, about four inches by six. My collection of BeeHive photos was a source of much pride. I used to take a route to school that meandered past a lot of different houses. When

I spotted a can of BeeHive Corn Syrup, I'd ask if I could have the label. If they didn't want to give it to me right then, I'd ask if I could have it when the can was empty. A few weeks later, I'd go back and gather up the label. Stamps cost three cents at the time, so I did odd jobs to earn enough money for postage. It was worth it.

With only 120 players in the league, I had 180 pictures. Every time you sent a request and they didn't have the player you wanted, you'd get a photo of Turk Broda instead. He was Toronto's goalie starting around 1935 or '36. I ended up trading a lot of Turk Brodas for other players to fill out my collection. I would stare at those pictures and wonder if someday a kid would ask for a BeeHive photo of Gordie Howe. Sitting in our drafty little house in Saskatoon, that seemed a million miles away. I couldn't know it at the time, but I'd end up realizing those childhood dreams much sooner than I ever would have dared to guess. And when I did arrive in the NHL, would you believe who I scored my first goal against? Turk Broda.

*Three*

# JUNIOR HOCKEY

My first training camp came in 1943, when I was only fifteen. With so many NHL players serving in the war effort, teams were searching high and low for prospects who could fill in. The Howe family, like so many across the country, knew more than we would have liked to about that war. I'm pretty sure my mother didn't get a decent night's sleep until my brothers Norm and Vern returned home safely. Despite the uncertainty of the time, NHL teams managed to keep playing a full fifty-game schedule. But they did have extra roster spots to fill, which meant a lot of young players got a look earlier than they might have otherwise. Quite a few even broke into the league during those years. I wasn't among them quite yet, but the circumstances did allow for my first taste of the big leagues. I can't say it went as well as I would have liked.

Prairie boys must have played some good hockey back then, because with so many able-bodied men off fighting in the war,

NHL scouts became pretty familiar with cities, towns, and whistle-stops all over western Canada. A scout for the New York Rangers, Russ McCrory, watched me play that season and apparently liked what he saw. From what I heard later, I think a few different teams were interested in me at the time, but Mr. McCrory was the first to come by the house. We sat down and he talked to my parents while I mostly listened. The talk went on for a while as he explained what the New York Rangers could do for me and what it would be like to attend the team's training camp. In the end, he asked if I wanted to travel to Winnipeg later that summer, when the Rangers would be holding camp with players from the big club. I'd never set foot out of Saskatchewan and certainly hadn't been anywhere on my own. I was just a fifteen-year-old kid, and a shy one at that, but I loved hockey more than anything and the thought of skating with some of the best players in the world trumped my nervousness. I agreed to make the trip to Winnipeg and we'd see where things went from there.

Until that point, the farthest away from Saskatoon I'd ever been was Regina, about 150 miles south, and that was only once for a hockey game. It doesn't seem too far now, but when I'd gone there the year before it had felt like a world away. It was my first road trip with teammates and we were excited about it for weeks. What could be better than traveling with your friends to play hockey? Getting on the train to Winnipeg was different. I was alone on an overnight trip to another province more than five hundred miles away. When the train pulled into the station in Winnipeg, no one from the team was there to meet me. I asked for directions to the Marlborough Hotel, where they'd told me I was staying, and found my way over. My roommate was a goaltending prospect, but we didn't get to know each other very well. Early in camp, he took a puck in the mouth and that was it for him. I ended up staying alone, which didn't help the feelings of isolation that had already set in.

The Rangers held training camp at the Amphitheatre, a big old arena in Winnipeg that was knocked down in the mid-1950s and replaced by the Winnipeg Arena. Now even that's gone, and the Jets play in a new building downtown. On the first day of camp, I remember being nervous as I walked from the hotel to the Amphitheatre. My nerves didn't settle down once I got there. The first person I went to see after I signed in was the trainer, who handed out the equipment. All I'd brought with me were my skates, so I needed to be outfitted from top to bottom. To his frustration, I couldn't answer many of his questions. I didn't even know my size. When he asked what position I played, I said, "All of 'em," because it was true. I'd played goalie, defenseman, and forward. I don't know if he thought I was some kind of smart-ass or what, but he needed to get me out the door so he asked what position I'd *like* to play. I honestly didn't know why the Rangers had brought me in, so I told him defenseman. I was comfortable on the blue line and figured I'd have as good a shot playing there as anywhere else. After being on the right wing for so many decades, it's strange to think that my first tryout as a professional hockey player was on defense. After seeing the trainer, my day went only further downhill.

Growing up, we couldn't afford proper equipment, so I didn't know what to do with all of the pads and protectors I'd just been given. I sat on a bench in the dressing room with my gear on the floor in front of me and just stared at it for a while. I'd never worn a garter belt before, for one, so I didn't know what it was for or how to put it on. I was also too shy to ask. Some of the other younger prospects noticed and started hacking on me for just sitting there looking confused. I didn't like that too much. Who would? It reminded me of my younger days when kids would tease me at school. I just wanted to figure it all out and get on the ice, where I knew what I was doing. One of the veterans, Alf Pike, eventually came in and sat down across from me. It was a godsend at the time. I watched Alf and mirrored his every move. He put on his right shin pad and I put on my right shin pad. I've dressed the same way ever since.

Once I stepped onto the ice, I was able to calm down. You often hear athletes talk about the playing field being a refuge from anything else that might be going on. That might sound like a cliché, but it's the truth. It was certainly never truer for me than it was at the Rangers' camp. Everything else around me was foreign—the city, the players, the equipment—but hockey was still the same, and I remember the relief I felt when it was time to play. I also recall thinking that I was capable of skating with everyone in camp. That realization was a boost to my confidence that I took with me after I left. I wasn't the best guy there, but no one was doing anything that was beyond me. For a raw fifteen-year-old, everything at camp that was hockey related went as well as could be expected. Well, everything except for one incident, that is. During a scrimmage, an older player—Billy Warwick, if memory serves—was coming down the wing. I went low, stuck out my hip, and sent him for a ride almost into the seats. He ended up straddling the boards and he wasn't too happy about it. Lester Patrick, the Rangers' general manager, called me over and said, "You don't do that here." In the heat of the moment, I thought he was talking about how they played in Winnipeg. I replied, "I'm sorry, sir, I've never been here before." It wasn't until later that I realized he meant you don't hit your own teammates like that during practice. Looking back now, I'm not sure my answer was half bad. It was the truth, after all.

*I need to start with the people who made me who I am. Here I am with Colleen, who brought out the best in me, and my parents, Kate and Ab, who taught me the lessons I needed to make it.*

*I have been lucky, no doubt about it. A lot of things have changed over the years, but the important things always stay the same.*

*That's me back when I was playing in Omaha in 1947. When the NHL had only six teams, the minor leagues were full of very talented players. Back then, I was just focused on making it to the big leagues.*

*Here I am with my younger brother, Vic. It is a pretty special feeling to play against your brother on a frozen pond one day and in the NHL the next.*

Hockey is a fast, tough game, and my father taught me early not to take dirt from anyone. I dished out a few licks over the years (here I am giving a Soviet player a taste of Canadian-style hockey in Moscow in 1974), but I have taken a few myself. Here I am (above) getting some medical attention from trainer Lefty Wilson in 1961.

I have been called "Mr. Elbows" more than once, sometimes as a compliment, sometimes not. I'll say this, though. If everyone played with their elbows up, the game might be faster and possibly even cleaner.

I fell for Colleen the
moment I laid eyes on her
in the spring of 1951. She
was as comfortable on a
fishing trip as she was at a
formal event. She had my
back for many years, and I
miss her every day.

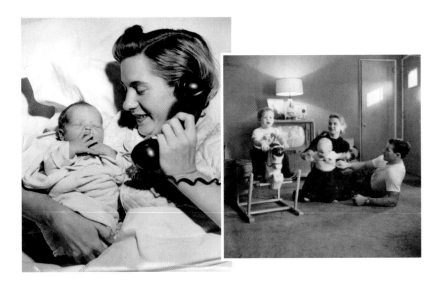

*Hockey players are on the road a lot, but I spent every minute I could with my family. Marty was born in 1954 (top left) and Mark came along the following year (top right). Cathy arrived in 1959, and Murray filled out the roster in 1960. Here we all are in the living room: from left to right, that's Marty, Murray, Cathy, Colleen, me, and Mark.*

*Hockey players love golf, and the Howes are no different. Here we are on the course with U.S. President Gerald Ford.*

*Here we all are at a family skating party.*

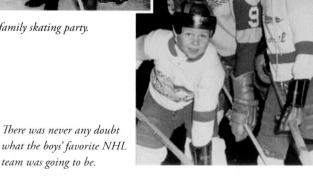

*There was never any doubt what the boys' favorite NHL team was going to be.*

I have always loved to fish, and I'll take any chance I can get to put a line in the water. Here I am fighting a marlin in Panama. Fishing is something we have enjoyed as a family since the kids were old enough to hold a rod, and we still like to get out on the water. Here I am in Florida with Mark.

We loved spending time as a family at Bear Lake, in Michigan. Colleen and I enjoyed racing sailboats on the lake—and you can tell by this photo who was the skipper in the family.

I loved my time in Detroit, and I would like to think I had a pretty special relationship with the fans there. My heart is definitely in Detroit. At the same time, I am very grateful for the chance to play in the WHA with Mark and Marty, which led back to the NHL. I loved my second career in professional hockey, though I never felt quite the same in green as I did in red.

When I wasn't playing hockey, Winnipeg didn't treat me that well. On the ice, I knew what I was doing. Off the ice, I missed home. For a kid who'd never really been away from Saskatoon or his family, nothing was easy or routine. I think about how shy I was then and wish I could go back to that time, put my arm around a young Gordie, and give him a few pointers. Even basic things like getting something to eat could cause me trouble. I remember that the Rangers had a training table set up at the hotel. Players would grab a plate and line up to eat buffet style. I was so nervous and awkward I couldn't bring myself to go to the buffet table. All of the big players from the team were there and I didn't want to bother anyone, so I just stood back and watched. No one was rude or shoved me out of the way, but we had only a short amount of time to eat and everyone needed to get down to business. As it happened, it was Alf Pike who realized I could use a hand. He pushed a few guys out of the way and told them that the kid needed to eat something as well. After I saw how things were done I felt more comfortable getting in there myself, but when you're shy, doing something for the first time can be especially tough. I've always thought it would be easier to be one of those people who doesn't worry about things like that, but that's just not me.

If I had been more outgoing at fifteen, there's a good chance I would have become a New York Ranger instead of spending more than a quarter of a century with the Detroit Red Wings. It's hard for me to imagine a different life, one in which Colleen and I raised our kids in New York City. A moment that almost made that a reality came later in camp, though. Frank Boucher, the team's coach, and Lester Patrick called me to their hotel room to talk about what came next. They liked enough of what they'd seen to sign me to a "C" form. At that time, the NHL had three types of contracts for prospects, known as "A," "B," and "C" forms. They were a sweet deal for the teams, but not so great for a player. A "C" form essentially gave your rights to the club that signed you. They told you where to play and they could renew the agreement every year for as long as they wanted. If you eventually did sign a proper contract, your salary and signing bonus were already determined in the "C" form, which really cut down a player's ability to negotiate early in his career.

Of course, I wasn't too concerned about contracts and "C" forms at the time. The Rangers also wanted me to attend Notre Dame, a Catholic school in Wilcox, Saskatchewan, that was known for turning out good hockey players. It's a tradition that has lasted. A long list of current and former NHL players went to school there. As it happened, I'm not one of them. I wasn't Catholic, so my first thought was that Notre Dame would be a bad fit. My next thought was about home. I'd only been in Winnipeg for a short time, but I didn't like feeling so alone. The thought of living at a boarding school, and a strict one at that, where I wouldn't know anyone didn't sound good at all. The school is about twenty-five miles south of Regina, which felt like a long way from Saskatoon. I didn't want to go to Notre Dame and I didn't want to sign anything with the Rangers, so I listened to their offer and told them thank you very much, but that I really just wanted to go home. They pressed me a bit, but my mind was made up. When I left for my return trip to Saskatoon, I remained a free agent. It turned out to be the right move.

That said, my lack of formal education has bothered me ever since. Notre Dame is a fine school and I know I would have learned a lot there. I enjoyed a long career as a hockey player and I don't have many regrets, but I do wish I had gone to school for a few more years when I'd had the chance. As it played out, though, I was happy to leave camp and head home. That fall, I was back in school in Saskatoon, and by winter I was once again skating on hometown ice, playing hockey with my friends.

During the 1943–44 season, scouts began to take more of an interest in what I was doing on the ice. I was still only fifteen, but I guess they started seeing me as a pretty good prospect. A number of teams sent letters and telegrams to our house, wanting to talk about a contract. In the middle of World War II those telegrams weren't great for a jittery mother with two sons fighting overseas, Norm in the navy and Vern in the army. Every time one arrived her mind jumped to the worst conclusion. My dad eventually put a stop to it. He told the teams to quit writing. If they wanted to talk about my hockey career, they'd have to come by the house and do it in person. That's how Fred Pinckney ended up in our parlor.

Mr. Pinckney was the timekeeper for the Saskatoon Quakers and a part-time scout for the Detroit Red Wings. He'd been watching me for a few years, and as my sixteenth birthday approached, his interest really began to pick up. Just as Mr. McCrory had done a year earlier, Mr. Pinckney came to the house, but he talked about why I should join the Red Wings. He made good enough sense, but I was hesitant to sign the "C" form he'd brought in his pocket. Two clubs were showing serious interest in me, the Rangers and the Red Wings, and I didn't know how to pick between them. My memory of the loneliness I'd felt the year before in Winnipeg also didn't make the thought of another training camp too inviting (added to which, this one was even farther away, in Windsor, Ontario). I asked Mr. Pinckney if anyone I knew was going. He said there would be a couple dozen guys from the area, including a bunch from Saskatoon. The idea of traveling to Windsor, which is just across the border from Detroit, with my friends seemed more appealing to me than being in Winnipeg by myself. After some more talk, I signed the form and agreed to attend training camp with the Red Wings.

When fall came, I boarded a train that would take me to my second professional training camp. Enough of us were making the trip that we filled an entire sleeper car. I'd say there were about twenty-two players in all, many of whom I'd played with and against for years. The trip took two days and two nights and sharing it with friends made me less anxious than I'd been the year before. Mr. Pinckney also went out of his way to make sure I made a good impression when I arrived in Windsor. He bought me the first suit I ever owned—jacket and pants, plus a coat, shoes, the works. He stuck the train ticket to Windsor in the breast pocket of the coat along with a five-dollar bill so I'd have some spending money. It was a heck of nice thing to do for a poor kid from the Prairies. The outfit even included a nice hat, but I ended up giving it to the train porter as a tip. I figured he could use a fedora more than I could.

I felt different at the Red Wings training camp than I had with the Rangers the previous year. I was sixteen and, at that age, even a few months can make a big difference. I was still just a lanky kid, so my play wasn't as physical as it would eventually become, but my puck handling seemed to impress the coaches and overall I remember feeling good on the ice. Holding my own against NHL-level talent once again helped my confidence. It was only a few years earlier that I'd been collecting BeeHive photos of guys I was now skating against, players like Bill Quackenbush, Carl Liscombe, and Syd Howe. In a funny bit of happenstance, my first Peewee team, the one I made using Frank Shedden's equipment, was actually named after the Red Wings—teams adopted the names and colors of NHL franchises. I even ended up drawing Syd Howe's jersey, which was fine by me. There was no relation, but I liked the coincidence of getting to wear my own name on my uniform. Who would have thought that in just a few short years I'd be playing alongside Syd himself. My dreams were becoming a reality more quickly than I'd ever dared to imagine. Unlike a year earlier, though, I felt less like a fish out of water and much more like I belonged.

At the end of the two-week camp, Jack Adams, who was then the coach as well as the general manager, sat me down and asked if I'd join the team's junior club in Galt, Ontario. Once again I was hesitant to commit. I asked if I'd know any of the other guys going to Galt and he told me there would be a couple, which was a big selling point. I also wanted to go home and talk it over with my parents. He said that wasn't a problem, but that I should be sure to bring all of my clothes with me when I came back. That part was easy, since I really didn't have many clothes to speak of. I wasn't much of a negotiator at the time, but I did make one request before I signed—a Red Wings jacket. The players on the big club had these great team jackets and I really wanted one as well. My first reason was practical. I didn't have many clothes and I knew I'd wear that jacket all the time. The other was more psychological. If I signed with the Red Wings, the jacket would help me feel like part of the team. Mr. Adams said he'd get me one, and with that we closed the deal.

I spent a few days at home visiting family and friends before getting back on the train for the return trip to Ontario. I didn't know it at the time, but I'd spent my last winter in Saskatoon. The train ride was lonely and more like my trip to Winnipeg than the one I'd just taken to Windsor with my friends. I had a few long days to think about what I'd just signed up for. By the time the train pulled into Galt, which is about fifty miles southwest of Toronto, I can't say I was feeling too confident about my decision. I didn't have much of a clue about what was going to happen once we reached the station. I didn't have a place to stay, nor did I know anyone in Galt. Much to my relief, Al Murray, the team's coach, was waiting for me when I arrived. Instead of taking me into town, though, he hustled me back on the train and we headed straight to Windsor for an exhibition game. It was one of the few times that season that I'd play against real competition. Later, I'd find out that Detroit hadn't been entirely honest with me.

I was told the club wasn't able to arrange a transfer from Saskatchewan to the Ontario Hockey Association (OHA), which meant I could play in exhibition but not regular league games. Mr. Adams wanted me to stay in Galt and practice with the team, though. By staying, I'd register as an easterner and be ready to go the next year. I figured that practicing with a junior team every day as opposed to returning to Saskatoon would do more to develop my skills, so I stayed even though it meant sitting out the entire season. I learned later that Detroit gave me only part of the story. At the time, the OHA allowed a club to transfer only three players from the west in any one year. The Galt Red Wings already had two transfers and apparently the third choice was between me and Terry Cavanagh, who was a few years older and a left winger. Terry and I were friends and we ended up living together in Galt in a boarding house. (Years later, he became the mayor of Edmonton.) The club picked Terry over me. I don't know if my decision would have been different had I known the whole story, but to this day I still don't appreciate being told a half-truth. What's more, after I missed an entire hockey season, Mr. Adams still didn't deliver on the team jacket as promised.

My sole purpose for being in Galt was hockey. On that score, I guess you could consider my time there a success. Although I did become a better player, to my deep regret I didn't accomplish much else. I'd planned to attend high school in Galt, but things didn't work out that way. On my first day in Galt, I walked over to the school to register, but as I approached the building I started to get cold feet. I meant to go inside, but seeing the kids talking to each other on the lawn in front of the school made me feel like an outsider. Meeting new people was awkward for me and I wasn't the best student, so in that moment I decided to be somewhere else.

I walked past the school until I hit the railroad tracks. From there I went into the first big factory I saw and asked if there were any jobs available. At the time, Galt Metal Industries was busy with contracts for the war effort, so they had plenty of work. Since I was still a minor, though, they needed to have someone from the hockey club vouch for me. When they called, a team official told them if I wanted to work, they should let me work. That's how easy it was for me to quit school and end up working in a metal factory. I started out spot welding and grinding parts that were used for the Mosquito bomber. I must have done pretty well, because they promoted me to inspector. Over at Plant 2, I worked on trench mortar shells. I'd put them in a vise and ream out all the burrs. They also gave me a micrometer to take readings. I didn't know how to use it, so I scratched a line on the glass where the needle should be. I was pretty good at the work and I enjoyed doing it. As an inspector, I'd walk around making sure the machines worked properly. If they were off, it was my job to shut them down. I felt a sense of responsibility to do the job well. What if the fins were wrong on a mortar that a Canadian soldier used overseas? I made sure nothing like that would happen on my watch.

My days in Galt settled into a steady routine. I'd work, go down to the rink to practice with the team, and go home. The job was fine and I enjoyed practicing, but it would be a lie to say I'm not bitter about the Galt club's lack of care regarding my schooling. It was my choice, but what does a sixteen-year-old understand about the ramifications of that type of decision? Growing up during the Depression, everyone in my family needed to earn money and working was what I knew. I wish that someone in the organization had looked out for my best interests.

I consider walking away from school that day to be the biggest mistake of my life. Since then, I've always advised young people to stay in school for the full shot, even if I didn't know enough at the time to do so myself. Eventually, my education ended up coming through hockey. I learned a lot from the people I met and the places I saw, but it still wasn't a substitute for school. If I could change one thing from that time, I'd make it past the big tree in front of Galt Collegiate Institute and into the office to register.

The Galt Red Wings had a good team that year and I like to think I could have helped them win the league if I'd played. As it was, I got in about a hundred practices with the team, which was more organized hockey than I would have played back in Saskatoon. Missing out on games was tough to handle, but in terms of hockey, my time in Galt was well spent. Outside of the rink, though, I still missed home. When I wasn't playing hockey or working I had little to do, so sometimes I'd find myself at the train station when I knew that Jack Adams and the Red Wings were scheduled to pass through town. I'd walk over there by myself and hope the train would stop. If it did, I figured I could board and ask Mr. Adams about my jacket. I wanted it badly that whole year, but Mr. Adams didn't deliver. I came through on my part of the deal by going to Galt, so I thought it was only right that he hold up his end. The train always just rolled through town, though, leaving me with little else to do but walk home.

When I went back to Windsor for training camp in 1945, I was feeling better than ever about my chances of making the NHL. I was still a lanky kid, fifteen or twenty pounds under my eventual playing weight, but I was seventeen and starting to fill out. After I scored a couple of goals in an exhibition game, Mr. Adams called me to his hotel room to talk about taking the next step in my career. The Galt Red Wings were an amateur club and he felt it was time for me to turn professional. His contract offer for the season was $2200 plus a $500 signing bonus. It was a pretty standard offer for a first contract at the time. I wasn't much of a negotiator and $2700 was a lot of money to me, but I did have one outstanding issue I needed to clear up. I told Mr. Adams that I wasn't sure I wanted to sign, since he had broken his word about the jacket. He laughed and assured me that I'd get a jacket. I signed the deal and Mr. Adams sent me to Omaha, Nebraska, to play on the Red Wings' farm team in the old United States Hockey League (USHL).

In Omaha we played in the Ak-Sar-Ben Coliseum, which is Nebraska spelled backward. We were the Omaha Ak-Sar-Ben Knights, often shortened to just the Ak-Sar-Ben. The USHL was a bus league, and we rode around the country playing teams as far away as Dallas to the south and Minneapolis to the north. The road trips could be long, but I didn't mind. I was playing professional hockey, which is all I ever wanted to do. Just as it did in Galt, my life in Omaha revolved around the sport. I remember that I went on only one date while I was there. A teammate was taking out a girl who looked like Elizabeth Taylor with a friend who would only go out on double dates. I was roped into it as a favor to my buddy, but it didn't go anywhere. I was just a shy kid and too consumed with hockey to worry about much else. I wanted to learn everything I could about the game and didn't see the point of cultivating a social life. Out of the $2700 I signed for when I was seventeen, I saved $1700. For a kid who used to sell fish for ten cents a pop at the back door of a Chinese restaurant, I figured I was doing okay.

The start of the season was slow going for me. Tommy Ivan, who would later coach me in Detroit, figured that young players were best served by sitting on the bench and watching. I didn't get many shifts to start out, and I was chafing at the lack of ice time. I was still learning about the game, though, and a few pieces of advice I picked up during those days have served me well since then. One day Carson Cooper, Detroit's chief scout, took me aside and told me to draw an imaginary line about twenty feet from the side boards and stay there. He told me that was my territory. I kept that in mind my entire career. The other piece of veteran wisdom that helped in those early days came from Joe Carveth, a right winger with the big club. He told me not to worry too much if I struggled out of the gate. It was all part of the learning process, he said, and once I settled down, the second half of the season would be much better. I tried to remember that as I was stuck on the bench. It took a little nudge on my part, but it turned out Joe was right.

One night we were playing in Dallas when my roommate started to get into it with the other team and the gloves came off. I knew the guy he was fighting from Saskatoon. He was big, but I didn't think he was that tough. He was really giving it to my roommate, though. I couldn't take just sitting there and watching, so I jumped over the boards and nailed the guy. After I served my penalty for fighting, Tommy Ivan looked down at me and asked, "What's the matter, don't you like him?"

I looked at him and said, "I don't like any of them." After that, I didn't miss another shift in Omaha.

I ended the season with 22 goals and 26 assists. When I was on the ice I also ran pretty much everything that moved, which led to scraps with nearly every tough guy in the league. At the time I figured if knocking guys around would punch my ticket to the NHL, then that's exactly what I would do. It took me a while longer to learn that you don't win many games from the penalty box.

The next step up the ladder for a prospect from Omaha was Detroit's number-one farm team, the Indianapolis Capitals of the American Hockey League. I never made it to Indianapolis, though. At the end of the season, Tommy Ivan sat down with Jack Adams to talk about my future. They agreed that I wasn't cut out for the minor leagues. I was eighteen years old and about to get the call to the NHL.

# Four

# ARRIVING IN DETROIT

If I say that today's players have it easy, I know I'll just sound like an old curmudgeon. I'm not exactly one for standing on my front porch and shaking a fist at the neighborhood kids, but I am in my eighties now, so if the shoe fits I might as well wear it. As I see it, the current generation of players can be pretty tough on the ice, but they definitely have things easier than we did once they're off it. Away from the rink, a player's life nowadays is pretty uptown. Salaries are in the millions and players live in fancy houses, drive fast cars, and fly to away games on private jets. It's a far cry from how we lived in the 1940s. I'm not complaining, though. We got to play hockey for a living in the best league in the world, but beyond that the average player's day-to-day life wasn't nearly as glamorous as it is now.

Detroit's training camp in 1946, before my first NHL season, is a case in point. The team decided to finish up camp in Detroit at Olympia Stadium. I loved that old barn. It was less than twenty years old at the time, but management didn't invest in its upkeep as much as they needed to, so the building was starting to show signs of wear and tear. When camp moved to Detroit, Jack Adams told us that accommodations were tough to find near the arena, so he set up cots for the rookies in the corridors below the stands. I can't imagine that sleeping on an army cot in a cold arena would go over that well with today's players, but that's exactly what we did. I think the arrangement suited Mr. Adams just fine. Not only did it save the club money, but there were curfews and bed checks, so he knew exactly where his players were at all times.

The first night at the Olympia we fell asleep easily enough, but we woke up in the middle of the night to little scratching sounds. Someone flicked on the lights and you can probably guess what we saw scurrying around on the floor. Rats. Big Detroit-sized rink rats that lived on the popcorn and other food that fans dropped beneath the stands. We jumped up, grabbed some hockey sticks, and started smacking the rats like crazy. They were likely even more upset about the situation than we were. Until we showed up, the Olympia was probably like an all-night smorgasbord. We slept with sticks next to our beds for the rest of the camp. When someone hit the lights, you'd wake up, grab your stick, and start swinging at those rats for all you were worth. Between us, we ended up getting quite a few, but I quickly learned that rats in the city are sort of like mosquitoes in the country. It doesn't matter how many you kill, because it's a battle you're never going to win.

One thing I can say with confidence about the difference between my early years in the league and today's NHL: These days, rookies probably aren't waking up in the middle of the night to kill rodents with their sticks. Having played in both eras, I can say that's a change for the better. Of course, there are also much more significant differences between then and now. How contracts are signed, for one. Standard operating procedure these days involves agents and lawyers and team officials with business degrees hanging on their office walls. Back then, all of the Detroit Red Wings contracts were signed in a face-to-face meeting between Mr. Adams and the player. When I sat down with Mr. Adams to sign my second professional contract, we were still at least a couple of decades away from the arrival of agents and management companies.

I knew that getting promoted to the big club would mean a serious step up in pay from my minor league contract. When Mr. Adams pushed the paper across his desk, it turned out to be a one-year deal for $5000. That was nearly twice as much as I'd made the year before and more money than my dad had ever made in a single year in his life. To be honest, I wanted to play so badly I probably would have signed any offer passed my way. This one turned out to be a fairly standard rookie deal for the time, right down to a minor league clause. It stipulated that if the Red Wings saw fit to send me down to Indianapolis at any time during the season, my salary would be chopped to $3500. The thought terrified me. As much as I didn't like the clause, it did provide some extra motivation. I didn't want to go back down to the minors and I sure as heck didn't want to lose out on all that money. I made a vow that I'd do whatever it took to stay with the club. The Red Wings kept me around for the whole year, but I worried incessantly about the possibility of being sent down. Thankfully, it was the only time one of my contracts had that type of stipulation.

During those years, Mr. Adams held most of the cards when contract negotiations came around. Not only did he have years of experience cutting deals with players but also, in my case, he was sitting across from an eighteen-year-old kid who wanted to play hockey for his team more than anything. Not exactly a position of strength for yours truly. At the time, the owners had the players over a barrel and they knew it. With six teams in the league, there were only about 120 jobs to be had at any given time. Every player in the NHL, including the stars, knew that there were guys champing at the bit to take his spot. Also, players were kept largely in the dark about team finances. We didn't know how much money franchises were making or losing, and even if we had, it wouldn't have meant much to most of us. Hockey was what we knew best. The owners and team officials, on the other hand, knew about the business side of the game. A lot of years passed and many things had to change before players figured out how to balance the scales more in our favor.

As much as I wanted to play for the Red Wings, I did screw up my courage enough to press Mr. Adams on one point. I thought about all of those nights I'd walked down to meet the train in Galt, hoping it would stop so I could see about my jacket. I also remembered all the times I'd walked back to my boarding house, disappointed that the train had just kept rolling through town. Before I signed the deal, I told him he'd have to deliver on his promise and get me a jacket. Once again, he chuckled, but this time he came through. I guess he didn't want to risk losing a decent prospect over the cost of a coat. He directed me to a downtown store and told me to go in, pick out a jacket, and sign for it. I went with Marty Pavelich and Ted Lindsay. The jacket I got had big, heavy slit pockets. The material was smooth on the outside, like satin, and it had leather sleeves with alpaca lining. It also had a big "D" with "Red Wings" written on it. Every time I put on that sharp-looking jacket I felt a bit more like I belonged.

My first NHL game arrived on October 16, 1946. It was Detroit's home opener against the Maple Leafs. Under normal circumstances my nerves would really kick in before a game. Early in my career, I used to go so far as to eat steak in the morning and eggs in the afternoon. I'd get so nervous on game days that protein was the only thing I knew I could keep down. As the puck was about to drop in the biggest game of my life, though, I was uncharacteristically calm. I didn't see the need to get that worked up, since I was pretty sure I wasn't going to see much ice time. We went through warm-up and then lined up at the blue line for the national anthem—they didn't resurface the ice between warm-up and the game. The referee would just blow the whistle and the two teams would stand on their respective lines listening to the song. I was standing alongside my teammates only half paying attention to "The Star-Spangled Banner" (they didn't play the Canadian anthem at the time), but my mind wasn't really on hockey. I was actually thinking about cribbage. My roommates had introduced me to the game in Windsor during the first part of training camp. It had hooked me, but I was still in the early stages of figuring it out. After the anthem, we'd head over to the bench and Mr. Adams would bark out the starters. They'd skate back to the circle and everyone else would take a seat. I was still busy counting crib hands in my head (15–2, 15–4, 15–6) when I heard Mr. Adams yell, "Sid, Adam Brown, and Howe!" I had no clue I'd be on the top line. I didn't have enough time to get nervous before the puck dropped.

Our line played well that night. In the first period, Brown opened the scoring with a pass from Sid Abel. The Leafs tied it at 1–1 about halfway through the second. Not long after that, I was coming up the right wing when Sid passed the puck to Brown, who head-manned it to me around the Leafs' blue line. I got on top of the puck about ten feet in front of Turk Broda. In that moment I wasn't thinking about my collection of Broda BeeHive photos, I just wanted to find a way to beat him. Turk was stocky compared to today's goalies, but he could really move. I slapped at the puck and it went over his shoulder and into the net. It wasn't the prettiest goal I ever scored, but they all count.

Late in the third period, we found ourselves down 3–2. We yanked the goalie and Sid found a way to tie it up with little time left. Sid was always a clutch player. That night he managed to salvage us a tie. I didn't have high expectations for my career at that point. I just wanted to stick around for a full season so I could say that I played a year in the big leagues. After I scored, I thought I'd always be in the record books, at the very least. Going into the next game, I did assume that we'd played well enough that Mr. Adams would leave our line together for a while. Boy, was I wrong. If there was one thing I learned about Mr. Adams over the years, it was that just when you thought you knew what he was doing, he'd switch it up on you. He dropped me from that line and I saw the ice only sporadically from then on. It took nine more games to score my second goal and another eleven after that to notch my third.

As much as I hated being glued to the bench, my hockey education was coming along in leaps and bounds. I remember one time early in that first season I had Bruins goalie Frank Brimsek beat, but instead of burying the puck, I got cute and just slid it toward the net. Brimsek's nickname was "Mister Zero" and, of course, he reached out with his paddle and kept it out. He ended up being one of the first American-born player inducted into the Hockey Hall of Fame. Wherever they're born, NHL goalies, for the most part, are so good that if they can see the puck they'll save it. When I got back to the bench, Sid Abel told me as much. When you get an opportunity to score, he said, you drill the puck into the back of the net as hard as you can. Later that game I got another chance at Brimsek and didn't make the same mistake twice. I wired one by him, just like Sid told me to. I learned a lot from veterans that year, sometimes just by watching them. Sid, for instance, used to customize his sticks to help his feel. He'd sit in the dressing room with a rasp and round off the heel and toe of his blade, something he felt allowed for better puck control. I copied that trick and found it helped both my stickhandling and my shooting. Throughout that first year, I kept reminding myself of what Joe Carveth had told me in Omaha: The first half of the season might be rough, but things will eventually settle down. Once again, it turned out to be pretty good advice.

When I did make it onto the ice, I was determined to contribute however I could. I figured that if dropping the gloves was what got me from Omaha to Detroit, it would probably help keep me there as well. It's fair to say that early in my career I was so eager to make an impression, I didn't care who was in front of me. I took on all comers, even the Rocket himself. At the time, Maurice Richard was arguably the biggest star in the game. Hockey fans don't need me to run down his resumé, but it obviously stacks up against anyone's and then some. A couple of seasons earlier he'd become the first player to score 50 goals in 50 games. It took until the 1980s before anyone else (Mike Bossy and Wayne Gretzky) would match that feat. In 1946, I was just a no-name rookie, but I didn't care.

The Rocket might have been among the bigger guys in the league, but I was still a good size, even at eighteen. If anyone got into it with a teammate, I was going to look him up, and that's where my thinking stopped. I fought pretty much everyone I could in my first few trips through the league. Of course, that also meant I ended up becoming well acquainted with the penalty box.

I guess Mr. Adams eventually had his fill of playing short-handed because a rookie couldn't stay out of the box. One day, he called me into his office and sat me down for a talk. Well, it wasn't so much a talk as it was a lecture. He asked if my plan was to fight the whole league one player at a time. I didn't yet know the term "rhetorical question," but I was pretty sure Mr. Adams wasn't looking for an answer. He knew I could fight, he said. Now I needed to prove that I could play hockey. Years later, when I ran summer hockey camps, I'd echo that sentiment to the kids. Take it from someone with plenty of experience, I'd tell them: You don't win many games from the penalty box. Even after my talk with Mr. Adams I still wasn't exactly a candidate for the league's most gentlemanly player. Although I was fortunate enough to win a number of awards in my career, for some reason I never seemed to be up for the Lady Byng Trophy. I guess I didn't make too much of a case for myself most seasons. If I'm being perfectly honest, there may have even been a couple of times I got away with something that could have drawn a whistle. Maybe.

I played in 58 games that first season, scoring 7 goals and adding 15 assists. The totals weren't bad for a rookie, I guess. We finished fourth that year and lost to Toronto in the semifinals of the playoffs. During that series, Toronto tough guy Gus Mortson and I weren't seeing eye to eye on much. Back then, teams shared the same penalty box. The setup wasn't always a good idea. We got chucked in there for fighting and, once there, figured we'd see if we couldn't resolve our differences. Our meeting of the minds quickly broke down and, as can happen, our scrap spilled out of the box and into the stands. A fan might have thrown a chair at Gus, at some point. I'm pretty sure the police showed up. They were a bit worried about the potential for a riot. That sounds a bit worse than it really was. "Riot" is a big word. If anything, it would have been only a little riot. As it was, the situation didn't get too out of hand. I respected what Mr. Adams said about fighting, but if it was a choice between that and sticking up for a teammate, then it seemed like an easy decision in my books. It wasn't the last time I got into it with Gus. We also had a bit of a dustup during the All-Star Game in 1948. Some people admonished us then, saying that fighting during an exhibition game designed to promote the league was inappropriate. In hindsight, they may have had a point. If I'm being honest, though, I still have to say that it felt like the right thing to do at the time.

In the off-season after my first year, I went back to Saskatoon. I'd missed Saskatchewan and it was great to come home. I spent time with family and friends, worked with my dad to stay in shape, and, of course, played baseball. As much as I enjoyed returning to my hometown for the summer, I remember that the best part was knowing that in a few months I'd be back playing hockey. My willingness to return to Detroit was a far cry from how things had been a few years earlier, when I wasn't sure I wanted to leave Saskatoon at all. But I was now nineteen and playing professional hockey for the Detroit Red Wings. I couldn't wait for the next season to begin.

The first time I met Sid Abel, I was just a kid. He was playing for Moose Jaw and had come up to Saskatoon to play our hometown boys. When the bus pulled up, I asked him if I could carry his skates into the arena. It was a trick I used to get through the doors for free. Sid was good to me. He handed over his skates and we went inside. If my life story was a movie, it might seem a bit corny that the kind-hearted hockey player would one day become linemates with the ragamuffin rink rat from Saskatchewan. But at the beginning of the 1947–48 season, that's exactly what happened.

Tommy Ivan, my old coach from Omaha, had been promoted to the big club. It was quite a shock to those who figured Mr. Adams would never cede control of the Red Wings. Until then, he was the only coach the team had ever known. But Tommy was a special case. He was just a little guy, but you wouldn't know it by talking to him. He was quiet and serious and, when he looked at you, he felt much bigger than five foot five. His playing career didn't amount to much, but he found his calling in coaching. Mr. Adams thought a lot of Tommy and moved him through the Red Wings system from Galt to Omaha to Indianapolis and then up to Detroit. I guess Mr. Adams felt he'd finally found someone he could trust with his hockey club. He moved into the front office full time and Tommy took over behind the bench. I think he was pretty happy with the spot he stepped into. We had Sid Abel, Ted Lindsay, Jim McFadden, Red Kelly, Marty Pavelich, Jack Stewart, Gerry Couture, Jim Conacher, Bill Quackenbush, Pete Horeck, Don Morrison, and Ed Bruneteau, among others. Not to mention a solid young goaltender, Harry Lumley, between the pipes.

On paper, we felt like our team was loaded with good players. When we hit the ice, it turned out we were right. I was still the baby of the team at nineteen, but Marty Pavelich and Red Kelly, who joined us from Galt and St. Mike's, were only twenty. Add in Lindsay, who was twenty-two, and it was nice to be with guys around my own age. We knew that combining our young corps of players with veterans like Abel set us up well not only for that season but also for years to come. In terms of my own career, the biggest move Tommy made that year was shuffling the lines around and putting me with Sid Abel and Ted Lindsay. It was a match made in heaven as far as I was concerned. The newspapers ended up calling us the "Production Line." I didn't know if it was because of the goals we scored or if it was a nod to Detroit's auto industry. Maybe it was both. Either way, we became the team's top line, with Sid at centre, me at right wing, and Ted on the left.

Sid, who was already a great player, seemed to know exactly where both Ted and I wanted to be. That might sound like a cliché, but it's true. He had a real knack for seeing how a play was about to develop before it happened. Younger fans have probably heard the same thing said about players like Wayne Gretzky and Sidney Crosby. Well, Sid could anticipate a play in the same way. Our line clicked from the beginning, but we didn't take it for granted. After practices, we spent countless hours running extra drills to improve on our natural chemistry. Once you reach the NHL, or become a professional in any sport, you learn that there's a fine line between the top players and the average ones. If you want to make a real difference on the ice, you need to put in the work. I think the same probably holds true for players in any league, at any age. The repetitions we put ourselves through were endless. I can't count the number of pucks Ted and I shot at Sid, who worked at finding just the right angles to tip them into the net. Looking back now, it's satisfying to think about how our near-constant drills eventually paid off in games.

Our line finished one-three-four in team scoring that year. Ted led the way with 33 goals and 19 assists. Jim McFadden came in second with 24 goals and 24 assists. Sid and I were next in line with 44 points each, me with 16 goals and him with 14. Earlier in that season I also switched to wearing the number 9. When I joined the Red Wings, it had been Roy Conacher's sweater, but he was dealt away near the beginning of the 1947–48 season. I didn't mind wearing number 17, except for one thing. We traveled to away games by train. On overnight trips, the sleeper cars had twenty-four berths, a dozen spots on top and twelve down below. Bunks were assigned by sweater number, with lower digits getting the bottom beds. A trainer pointed out to me that by switching numbers I could get a lower berth and sleep more comfortably. I snatched up Conacher's number straightaway. After spending most of my career as number 9, it feels strange to try to picture myself wearing a different number. It's funny to think that, at the time, it was purely a practical decision.

Our early season predictions of success ended up coming true by the end of the year. We jumped up to second place, just 5 points behind the Maple Leafs. Come playoff time, we took care of New York in six games to reach the Stanley Cup finals. Once there we met the Leafs, who were the defending champions. They still had a good team, anchored by Syl Apps, Teeder Kennedy, and Turk Broda in net. As usual, they were a tight-checking, disciplined bunch. The experienced players in blue ended up trumping the young talent in red, beating us in four straight. But that's the way hockey works. First you learn to play, then you learn to win.

The next year we put another good team on the ice. It was my third year in the league and the Production Line was starting to get rolling. Sid won the Hart Trophy as the league's most valuable player and was named to the first All-Star team, along with defenseman Jack Stewart, while Ted and I were both named as Second Team All-Stars. I was fortunate to be selected despite fighting through a knee injury that season. In December, I had surgery to repair some torn cartilage, which cost me twenty games. Being on the shelf is always depressing, but in retrospect I can't complain too much. It turned out to be the most games I ever missed in any one stretch in my career. I certainly had my share of injuries over the years, but I was lucky enough to play through most of them. After returning to the ice, I was eager to make up for lost time. I went on a bit of a tear to end the season, finishing with 12 goals and 25 assists in 40 games. The Red Wings topped the league in points for the first time since I'd joined the team in what would turn out to be seven straight seasons. As we headed into the playoffs, we felt as if momentum was on our side. For a while, it looked like it was. We beat Montreal in a tough seven-game series, which once again put us in the finals against the Maple Leafs. They'd had a rockier season that year, finishing fourth overall. Still, those damn Leafs managed to turn it on in the playoffs. They swept us in four games straight again. It was their third Stanley Cup in a row and we were sick of it. Getting swept once was bad enough, but having it happen in back-to-back years was like a punch to the gut. We were a proud group, and as we sat in the dressing room after our final loss of the season, we promised each other the next year would be different.

In 1949–50 we were on a mission. The taste of what it was like to play in the Stanley Cup finals was still fresh, and we knew we were good enough to finish the job. That season we again won the league championship, finishing 11 points clear of Montreal. I was twenty-one years old. It was my fourth year in the league and I felt like I'd turned the corner from being a raw kid with some ability into a more complete hockey player. That year, the NHL also expanded the schedule to seventy games from sixty, which was fine by us. The members of the Production Line, who finished one-two-three in scoring, were happy to play as many games as we could. Ted led the way with 23 goals and 55 assists for 78 points. He also had 141 penalty minutes, more than twice as many as I was whistled at for that year. Sid was next, with 34 goals and 35 assists for 69 points, and I was one point behind him, notching 35 goals and 33 assists. My total that season was three points ahead of the Rocket, who finished fourth. Ted and Sid were picked as First Team All-Stars, while I was named to the second team along with teammates Red Kelly and Leo Reise Jr. Out of ten spots on the All-Star Team, five were filled by Red Wings. By the time the playoffs came around, we were certain that our talent was now steeped in enough experience to go all the way.

The playoffs started on March 28, 1950. It was just three days before I turned twenty-two, but my birthday couldn't have been further from my mind. We'd drawn the Leafs in the semifinals, which was fine with us. We were hungry for another crack at them after our previous playoff exits. As it happens, though, the best-laid plans often don't work out the way you'd like. Once the puck dropped, game one was like déjà vu. The Leafs jumped out to a quick lead and were up 3–0 in the second period.

What happened next stirred up a controversy that lasted for years to come. Partway through the second period, Toronto center Teeder Kennedy was carrying the puck up his left wing. As I skated over to back-check, I was looking to anticipate his next move. I was closing in for the hit when I spotted the Leafs' Sid Smith going down the middle. I figured Kennedy would move the puck to Smitty, so I leaned forward with my stick to intercept the pass. I was coming in hard and the lean brought my face closer to the ice. When Kennedy followed through on his backhand, he caught me with his stick. I tried to close my eyes, but wasn't quick enough. I went into the boards headfirst at an awkward angle. Some Detroit fans at the Olympia that night swore that Kennedy had sticked me on purpose. Some said it was even a butt-end. As for Teeder, he was adamant that his stick just grazed me, if anything. He maintained that he was simply trying to avoid a check and I lost my balance. As I recollect it, I believe his stick hit me, but I don't blame him for it. He was just following through on a backhand and trying not to get hit. Hockey's a fast game and sometimes things happen.

I can't say I remember too much about what happened after I went into the boards. My teammates told me about it later, though. I've also seen the pictures, which aren't pretty. The trainers rushed out to find me unconscious and bleeding. They wrapped some bandages around my head and loaded me onto a stretcher. By all accounts, Coach Ivan and my teammates weren't having any of Teeder's apologies. They took some runs at him to even things up, and apparently the rest of the series was pretty rough. My injuries included a broken nose, a fractured cheekbone, and a badly scraped eyeball. Most worrisome, though, was a serious concussion. Complications that arose from the swelling in my brain meant that staying alive was a bit touch and go for a while.

I was conscious enough to remember the ambulance ride from the Olympia to Harper Hospital. It was horrible. Every time we turned a corner I felt like throwing up. They kept telling me I was okay, but I had a persistent sensation of falling that made me nauseous. When we reached the hospital, they rushed me inside for

X-rays. The prognosis wasn't good. Bleeding in my brain was causing pressure to build up in my skull. If it wasn't relieved, there was a chance I would end up dead. They called in a good neurosurgeon, Dr. Frederick Schreiber, and he opted to drain the fluid building up in my brain by drilling a hole in my head. I was prepped and on the operating table by about 1 A.M., ready for Dr. Schreiber to perform trephine surgery. A trephine is a medieval-looking surgical instrument that resembles a corkscrew. Believe me, if you can avoid having a hole drilled in your skull by a trephine, I'd recommend it. I remember my head being strapped down to the operating table before they started. The only sensations I experienced during the procedure were the pressure and the noise. It's not a sound you want to hear. My most vivid memory from the ninety-minute operation is hoping they'd know when to stop. After it was done, they didn't want me to fall asleep (in case I didn't wake up, I suppose), so they kept pricking my foot with a needle to keep me awake.

From what I understand, radio stations across Canada kept people updated on my condition throughout the night. By the next morning, I was still in rough shape, but it looked like I was out of the woods. When they finally allowed me to sleep, I was out for an entire day. By the time I came around, Mr. Adams had arranged for my mother and my sister Gladys to come down from Saskatchewan. It was a surprise to see them in Detroit, but I was happy they were there. The trip was my mother's first airplane ride, and between that and her worrying about my injury, she was looking a bit the worse for wear. She was so pale that at one point I told her, "Oh hell, Mum. You take the bed." She laughed, and I think that seeing I was well enough to joke helped to ease her mind. In the days after my surgery, all sorts of cards and packages arrived from all over Canada and the U.S. I was touched that so many people cared about my well-being. I still am, in fact. With Gladys's help, I tried to respond to every person who took the time to send me something.

As close as I came to shuffling off into the sunset at the tender age of twenty-one, I bounced back relatively quickly from the surgery. To this day, I'm still surprised by the speed of my recovery. As serious as my injury was, the timing also meant that I didn't miss any regular season games. I was back on the ice and ready to go by the next training camp. The doctors did make me wear a leather helmet for a while, but I was so happy to be skating again that I agreed to it without much fuss. As for the Red Wings, they took care of business while I was in the hospital. It took seven games, but we finally beat the Leafs. In the Stanley Cup finals we were up against the Rangers, who had eliminated Montreal in five games in the other semifinals. It was a hard-fought series that went the distance. Pete Babando finally got the monkey off our backs when he scored in the second overtime of game seven. I was at the Olympia for the game and joined the celebration on the ice in my street clothes. I was happy we won, but I also remember feeling removed from the jubilation around me. I like to earn things, and I didn't feel like I'd contributed that much to the victory. That said, after years of knocking on the door, the Red Wings had finally broken through. It was our first Stanley Cup together. It wouldn't be our last.

*Five*

# COLLEEN JOFFA

To be a good hockey team, you need talented players. I know that's not exactly a profound insight, but it's true. Plucky teams without much skill can steal a few games here and there, but they rarely win anything that matters. Having said that, though, you can have all the talent in the world and still not get anywhere if players aren't willing to put the team ahead of themselves. A good team is just that: a good team. Great teams, without exception, are full of players who care more about the name on the front of their jersey than the one on its back. They come together less often than you might think.

Most professional hockey players have healthy egos. To be fair, they come by them honestly. As kids, they were always the best player on their teams. That all changes when they reach the big leagues and the talent around them catches up. At that point, some guys just can't bring themselves to accept a lesser role, and they're the ones who can turn a winning team into an also-ran. It doesn't matter if it's the NHL or your local beer league, some guys won't ever understand that the whole is greater than the sum of its parts. They might hog the puck or refuse to back-check. Maybe they chase their own statistics. The really frustrating ones do all of the above and more. The ways in which an otherwise skilled player can choose to play losing hockey are endless. The same holds true across all team sports. It could be hockey, basketball, football, or soccer; the modus operandi of a selfish teammate is the same. For a professional, the motivation to look out for number one is easy enough to understand. During contract negotiations, goals and assists speak more loudly than the number of times you gave up your body to block a slap shot. Regardless of the size of your paycheck, though, your teammates always know who's in it for the right reasons and who's not.

In the early 1950s, I played with a rare group of guys who put the team ahead of themselves. It began with stars like Sid Abel and Ted Lindsay and carried all the way down the roster. In those years, there's no question that the Red Wings were stocked with talent, but that wasn't why we won. The reasons went beyond our skill on the ice. We were a close-knit bunch who played for each other as much as anything else. You never wanted to look down the bench at your buddy and know that you'd let him down. In the third period, when the game is on the line and you're dog-tired at the end of a shift, that can be why you dig deeper for the last ounce of energy left in your legs. Winning a championship takes a whole team willing to pay the same price on every shift. The opposite is also true. If you don't care about your teammates, maybe you don't dig in to get back into position to take away an odd man rush. Maybe you lose focus and that's the instant your check slips behind you and tips the puck into the net. The NHL game moves so quickly that a single mistake can be the difference between winning and losing.

The only NHL locker room I knew at that time was Detroit's, but when players were traded to our club they'd always remark on how close we were. Every team I played on wasn't the same way, but in those days we were like a family. It was a special team and I still feel lucky to have been a part of it. Looking back, I can see that our camaraderie wasn't an accident. We didn't just go our separate ways after practice. The younger guys, especially, spent all kinds of time together. We ate meals together, went to church, played cards, went bowling, chased girls, and many of us even lived under the same roofs.

I can't imagine that young Detroit players would go for a similar arrangement these days, but back then most of the Red Wing bachelors lived together in rooming houses organized by the team. In my first few years in Detroit I lived at Ma Shaw's place. It was an old brick house only a few blocks from Olympia Stadium. When I first arrived, my roommates were Ted Lindsay, Jack Stewart, and Harry Lumley. The rooms would turn over periodically, usually when someone got hitched or, more likely, was dealt away by Trader Jack, as deal-happy a general manager as you'll find. My spot in Ma Shaw's house opened up when Bill Quackenbush left. Other guys stayed at rooming houses run by Ma Tannahill and the Michaud brothers. I was happy at Ma Shaw's.

Nowadays, rookies can afford to live wherever they choose with the money they make on their first contract. Not us. We made okay money, particularly if there was no family to support, but every dollar counted. The sports world was still decades away from athletes becoming instant millionaires when they turned professional. It was certainly a different time, but in many ways it suited me just fine. I was still just a teenager when I moved to downtown Detroit. My stops in Galt and Omaha had given me a taste of living away from home, but I still wasn't that far removed from the Saskatchewan prairie. When I wasn't at the rink, big city living still felt foreign to me.

From a practical perspective, living so close to the arena was great. I was always just a hop, skip, and a jump from being on the ice. In the years since, I've often wished I still had that same commute to work. I'm sure Mr. Adams also liked having so many of his players living in the shadow of the arena. He preached about the need to stay focused on the game, so he probably figured that the Olympia served as a great visual aid. Personally, I liked having my teammates around for company. When I was eighteen, especially, going home to an empty apartment every day after practice would have been depressing. Most teenagers would rather spend time with friends than be alone, and I was no different. Living at Ma Shaw's meant that someone who was also at loose ends was always around. It was probably similar to living in a college dormitory. For a long time my roommates at Ma Shaw's were Ted Lindsay, Red Kelly, and Marty Pavelich. When Metro Prystai was traded to the Wings, the five us lived together for quite a while.

For entertainment we'd often just sit around and play cards. Nothing too fancy, just low-stakes games of cribbage, hearts, or pinochle for a penny a point. It wasn't until later in life that I became hooked on bridge. I even played a few hands with Charles Goren, once. (For a bridge player, it was a big deal sitting down with Goren, who wrote books on the game and had a column in *Sports Illustrated*.) The life of a professional hockey player, when you're not at practice or on the road, is chock-full of free time. We spent a lot of time eating, going to the movies, or bowling. Some guys even went ballroom dancing. I didn't join in, but I'd occasionally tag along to watch. Dancing the tango and fox-trot may not seem like a fitting outing for a bunch of hockey players, but it was an entertaining pastime. It also helps to be athletic when dancing, which appealed to some of the guys. Some of them improved to the point where they weren't half bad. As well, dance halls and pretty girls usually went hand in hand, which, to be honest, provided most of the appeal in the first place. When it came to chatting up girls I was quite shy, but many of my teammates sure weren't. They collected a lot of numbers and took all sorts of girls out on the town. I went on my share of dates, but it was nothing compared to some of the guys.

When I roomed with Metro Prystai, I used to get him in trouble every once in a while just for a laugh. He had this deep growl of a voice, and for some reason I could do a fairly spot-on imitation. At that age, nothing's better than playing a good practical joke on your buddy and my Metro impression came in handy. When a girl would call him up, sometimes one of the guys would pass the phone to me. Instead of getting some sweet nothings from Metro, she would hear me deliver a gravelly, "Whaddya want?" After talking to her for a while, my capper would be along the lines of, "Listen, you broads gotta stop calling here." The girl, of course, would slam the phone down right away. When (or if) Metro saw her again, he'd have to do some fast talking to patch things up. It probably wasn't the nicest joke to play on the girl or my friend. Then again, Metro could always find himself a date, so I didn't feel like he ever went lonely because of me. Metro joined us in 1950 after Mr. Adams pulled off a big trade with the Black Hawks. We missed the guys who left, but we appreciated having Metro on our side. He could really put the puck in the net.

Metro was originally from Yorkton, Saskatchewan, which gave us a lot in common. A number of Red Wings in those years were from Saskatchewan, including Gerry Couture, Bill Folk, Tony Leswick, Joe Carveth, Sid Abel, and myself. My closest friend at that time, though, was Ted Lindsay, a tough kid from northern Ontario. He came from Kirkland Lake, a rugged mining town, which probably had a lot to do with his temperament. Hockey fans from that time know that Ted played the game like a holy terror. He had a reputation for not being the nicest guy in the league and it was probably fairly earned. There's not a pair of shoulders in the world big enough to hold the chip he carried around. Some have even described him as mean, and they might be right. Truth be told, he could be the same way off the ice, but I didn't see that side of him too often. At that time, I'd have to say I considered him the closest thing I had to family outside of Saskatoon. Ted was there for most of the significant moments in my life during those years, including the biggest of all. He was around when I met a pretty little blonde girl named Colleen Joffa.

The first time I laid eyes on Colleen was just before I turned twenty-three in the spring of 1951. To kill time, I used to wander to a bowling alley, the Lucky Strike, a few blocks from the Olympia. Sometimes I'd get a lane and other times I'd just watch other bowlers. I used to do a fair bit of people watching back then. Occasionally I'd just sit on a bench and check out the world going by. Detroit could be a pretty entertaining place if you stopped to pay attention. One night at the Lucky Strike I looked over and saw what had to be, quite possibly, the best-looking girl in the Midwest. Heck, maybe in the entire country. I was smitten. I don't know if it was love at first sight, but if it wasn't then it was pretty close. Of course, I was so shy at the time I didn't know what to do. Just rushing up and saying hello felt too forward. My parents had raised me to believe that when a young man had serious intentions for a girl, he should proceed with a certain amount of propriety. It took a few weeks before I decided to ask Joe Evans, the alley manager, for an introduction. I was at the lanes one night with Vic Stasiuk, a left winger who had just come over from the Black Hawks, when Joe introduced us.

Colleen had just finished high school and was working as a secretary before going to college. She was a sharp cookie, I could tell that right out of the gate. She also had a great voice that matched her looks. I offered her a ride home, but she had the family car that night so she turned me down. It was a small setback, but not enough to deter me. I convinced Joe to track down her number and a few days later I took a deep breath and dialed her up. Normally I wasn't one to stay on the phone for too long, but our first talk was a marathon. Three or four hours passed with hardly a pause, which was a record for me at the time. That is, until the next night, when we did it again. The night after that was the same thing. Talking to her was easy, but it still took me more than a week to ask her out. Years later, she told me she was wondering how big of a hint she needed to drop before I got a clue. Thankfully, I eventually wised up.

On our first date we went to a movie at the Michigan Theater in downtown Detroit, but I have no recollection of what was playing. I was too busy fretting over whether to put my arm around her to pay attention to what was happening on the screen. I don't think my arm ever got around her shoulders, but I'm pretty sure we held hands. Judging by our phone calls I knew she was interested, but I could tell she was hesitant. As it turns out, she'd been going steady with some baseball player through high school. When I came along, the ballplayer had shipped out for the summer, leaving her all by her lonesome in Detroit. His loss was my gain, as far as I was concerned. After the show, I took her to Carl's Chop House for dinner. It was a classic steak place that was a pillar of the Detroit dining scene for decades. It closed its doors a few years ago, I heard. What's happened to Detroit's economy has been tough to watch. I don't live there anymore, but as someone who loves the city, it's hard to see. I know a little something about comebacks, though, and I like to think that Detroit has one in store. The city has heart; that much I know for sure.

When we finished dinner at Carl's, we moved over to Seller's Restaurant and Lounge. I knew that Ted would be there with his girl, Pat, and I wanted them both to meet Colleen. I can't remember if Ted and Pat were engaged at that point or just going steady but, either way, they were married not long after. Colleen used to tell the story of the first time she remembered hearing my name. A year before we met, she was heading out the door to go to school when Budd, her stepdad, started talking about a hockey player who was almost killed in a game the night before. She felt terrible for this faceless player and thought it was awful that he might die over something as trivial as hockey. Of course, the article Budd was reading in the paper that morning was about our playoff game against the Leafs. It took until halfway through our first date before she realized I was the same dumb hockey player who'd smashed himself up on the boards.

As a kid, Colleen, much like me, didn't realize how little she had. Although she was raised in Michigan and I grew up in Saskatchewan, we were both children of the Depression. Times were tough all over. Her father was a twenty-eight-year-old musician who played swing music during the Big Band era when he married her mother, who was only seventeen at the time. Between the drinking and the philandering, he didn't exactly turn out to be husband of the year. Her mom left her father when Colleen was still very young. That's never an easy decision, but in those days raising a child as a single mother was especially tough. Instead of putting Colleen up for adoption, her mom leaned on her family for help. For a time, Colleen lived with her great-aunt Elsie and her uncle Hughie, who were big influences in her life, as was her grandmother. Her mother remarried when Colleen was twelve, which brought more stability to her home life. It didn't sound like the easiest childhood, but she never complained about it. She only talked about how much she loved her friends and family. She was grateful for the people in her life who had helped her along the way. It's something we shared.

Around the time I spotted Colleen in the bowling alley, I was hanging around in Detroit for a few weeks, waiting to go on a trip to Florida. Our season had ended in bitterly disappointing fashion. We'd had a great run in the regular season, finishing first overall with 101 points; it was the first time a club had topped the century mark. I led the league in scoring with 43 goals and 43 assists for 86 points, which was good enough for my first Art Ross Trophy. The total also put me 1 goal and 19 assists ahead of the Rocket, who finished second. He got his revenge in the playoffs, though, when Montreal eliminated us in six games in the semifinals. After steamrolling over everyone all season, it hurt to come up so short when it mattered most. In the Stanley Cup finals, Toronto ended up beating Montreal in a series that saw all five games go to overtime. Bill Barilko finally ended it on his famous flying goal. It was Toronto's fourth Stanley Cup in five years. The Leafs had established a dynasty, but deep down we still believed that the Red Wings were the team to beat.

After our failure in the playoffs, Ted, Marty Pavelich, Red Kelly, and I decided to take a vacation to regroup and get some sun. I'd been looking forward to the trip, but after my first date with Colleen I started having doubts about going. I wanted to squeeze in as much time with her as possible and so we went out every night until I left for Florida. On one of those early dates, I remember leaning over and asking how old she thought a guy should be to get married. We'd only known each other a few weeks, so she told me later that she didn't know what to make of the question. Was I serious, or was I just trying to score points? I'll say this much: I never put the question to any other girl. I also may have figured she had one too many guys knocking on her door. If I gave her something to think about, I was hoping it might put the brakes on the competition. Whatever she thought at the time, the reason I asked that question is perfectly clear to me. I loved her from the beginning.

By the time we left for Florida, I was in a bad way. We'd met only a few weeks earlier, but I missed Colleen like I'd known her my whole life. I couldn't tell any of this to my buddies, of course. Ted, in particular, would have been merciless if he'd known I was so lovestruck. I made time nearly every day to sneak away and write Colleen a quick note. The irony of seeing me struggle to share my feelings on paper wouldn't have been lost on my teachers back in Saskatoon. Poetic or not, I needed to let her know how much she meant to me. In her typical sweet way, Colleen saved all of my letters from those early days. Here are a few excerpts:

*April 15*

*Hollywood, Florida*

*Dear Colleen:*

*Hello honey, well we're not there as yet but already I've found out you can miss someone even though you know them but for a few days.*

*Love, Gord*

*April 17*

*Hollywood, Florida*

*. . . as soon as we get our tans we all intend to catch a few big fish. I'm really looking forward to that as I love to fish. There's only one thing I like more this last week and that's a little girl in Detroit.*

*Love, Gordie*

*April 19*

*Hollywood Beach, Florida*

*Hello love,*

*. . . all I can think of right now is as I've always thought for the past few days and that is "I wish you were down here also." Goodnight for now, dear.*

*Love, Gordon*

*April 20*

*Hollywood, Florida*

*. . . we intend leaving here the night of the 26th so we will be in Saturday sometime. I hope to stay awhile and spend a few days with you if I can. I would love to spend as many more nights with you as I can before heading for home. So how about telling everyone you are out some place starting the night of Saturday the 28th . . .*

*As always,*
*Love, Gordie*

*April 23*

*Hollywood Beach, Florida*

*. . . I really enjoyed my fish as we ate about 6:00 and I hadn't anything to eat, and believe it or not all I had was one beer all day. So you and I seem to be in the same boat, but that's the way I like it. 'Cause I think the world of the girl in my boat with me.*

*Love and stuff, Gordon*

Some of that might be a bit sappy, but it still brings back a lot of good memories. I wasn't exactly Shakespeare, but I wanted to let her know I'd be worth the wait. Unfortunately, we faced a number of hurdles in the early going that put a lot of pressure on my humble letter-writing skills. For one, I had to head back to Canada straight after returning from Florida. The government granted me only a temporary work visa, which barred me from spending any more time in the U.S., other than for brief visits. The border rules meant that Colleen and I wouldn't see each other until the team reconvened in the fall. I knew I was crazy about her, but since I was leaving she wasn't quite ready to commit. She said we hadn't known each other long enough to be exclusive, so I reluctantly agreed that we should date other people while I was gone. Being thousands of miles away from a girl you're falling for is a hard situation. Added to which, the ballplayer was still in the picture, and I didn't know what to think about that. Colleen was such a catch I also figured that Lord only knew how many other guys were lining up to ask her out while I was stuck in Saskatoon.

Young hockey players usually don't struggle to find a date. Girls always seem to be around if you're looking. Until that point, though, I'd never met anyone like Colleen. She had it all, as far as I was concerned. Not only was she smart and funny and beautiful, but I also felt completely comfortable around her from the first time we spoke. Any shy person can tell you that's not always the case. When I was in Omaha, I remember being so spooked by a girl that I actually crawled out of a window to avoid taking her out. She'd been coming to games for a few weeks and it was pretty clear she was interested in me. I lived about six blocks from the rink and when I'd walk home from games, she was often waiting in ambush. The fellas started to tease me whenever she came around. One day she confronted me and asked why I wouldn't take her out. I didn't know what to say. In an attempt to avoid dealing with the question, I told her I only liked girls with gray hair. It was a silly answer, but it seemed to do the trick in the moment. You had to hand it to this girl, though. She was persistent. After the next game, I was in the dressing room when the door swung open. There she was standing in the hallway with her hair dyed gray. The guys gave a big whoop when they saw her and started cracking up. I was so nervous I did the bravest thing I could think of. I pulled on the rest of my clothes and went out the back window. As soon as my feet touched the pavement outside, I took off in a dead sprint until I reached my front door. It goes without saying that meeting Colleen was an altogether different story. By the time I returned to Detroit after our first summer apart, she'd broken it off with the baseball player. Thank heavens for that small mercy. The road was clear for me to try to sweep her off her feet, but for a while I had trouble getting out of my own way.

As much as I wanted it to be smooth sailing, the first few months after I got back into town were choppy. I tried to spend as much time with Colleen as possible, but sometimes my team duties threw a wrench into that plan. For instance, the Red Wings would often schedule players to appear at functions or banquets. Sometimes the requests were last minute, but it didn't matter. When Mr. Adams told you to go somewhere, you went. We'd just come off the season's first big road trip and Colleen and I hadn't seen much of each other. We had a big date planned for after the team's first game back. It was on a Friday and Colleen was excited that she didn't have to worry about working the next day. Then disaster hit. The club decided to send me to a banquet that night. When I called Colleen to cancel, it's fair to say she wasn't at all happy and she let me know it.

After the banquet ended that night, a few of us decided to go out. One of my teammates wanted to swing by a concert to see a girl he was dating. We walked in toward the end of the show—the Four Freshmen were playing—and sat down with the girl and her friends. I looked over, and who was in the next booth? Colleen.

And she wasn't alone. I was crushed. I tried not to show it, but I'm sure the hangdog expression on my face was clear enough. After I broke off our plans that afternoon, an old boyfriend called her up and asked her to the show. She was so angry with me for canceling that she went. Here I was falling in love with this girl, and there she was in a booth cozying up to some other guy. It was a terrible moment.

We had a game the next night. Normally I would have called Colleen and told her there was a ticket waiting for her at the gate. I always sat her next to Ma Shaw, who came to all of our games. That day, I didn't call. Late in the afternoon, though, the phone rang and it was Colleen on the other end. It was a pretty brazen move for a girl in the early 1950s, but that was Colleen. She never had much use for convention if it didn't suit her. She had bought her own ticket for the game and wanted to know if we could meet up afterward. I said that would be fine, except that I had a date. I figured that two could play at whatever game she was up to. As it turned out, my date was a bust. I didn't think much of it at the time, but years later I found out that Colleen had a hand in muddying the waters. Once at the game, apparently she marched down the aisle to her regular seat and, in a loud voice, asked Ma Shaw to apologize to me for breaking our date that night, but something had come up. I'm sure Ma Shaw was mortified. One seat over, my date heard the message loud and clear. I'm sure it would have made Colleen happy to see how frosty she was to me later that night. I have to admit it was a clever trick. Colleen said it ate at her conscience for years until she finally confessed. I can't say I was upset when I heard the story. Colleen said she knew we'd make up and she wanted to make sure there weren't any complications when that happened. Turns out she was exactly right and we made up shortly after. I forgave her for not knowing about banquets and she forgave me for not knowing about women.

By the time I had to leave the country again the next spring, our relationship was on firmer footing, but there were still some uncertainties. Not seeing each other for months at a time would once again be tough. While insecurity had plagued me the previous summer, our second summer apart was harder for Colleen. Part of that was my fault. As much as I was falling in love, I was still shy when it came to writing letters. I kept a dictionary beside me to make sure my spelling didn't make me look like a donkey in her eyes. A few months into the off-season I went north to Waskesiu Lake to do some fishing and golfing, but I didn't have a dictionary there so my letters dried up. Sometimes absence can play funny tricks on the mind. When Colleen stopped hearing from me, she thought it was over. She even met someone else who fell pretty hard for her in a hurry. Lucky for me, I returned from the lake in time to head that nonsense off at the pass. I was shocked when she told me she thought I'd moved on. To fix the situation, I needed to do some fast talking. I told her I would have written more, but we had been in such a remote spot there wasn't a post office around. She accepted my explanation and we managed to put things back on the rails. Of course, when we went up to Waskesiu Lake years later, what was the first thing she saw? A post office. She said, "Oh look, they have a post office now." Naturally, I'd forgotten about my little white lie and I told her it had been there forever. She gave me a pretty hard whack on the shoulder and I wasn't even sure why. I probably deserved it.

In my defense, when I wasn't at the lake I did write to her that summer. Colleen, of course, saved the letters.

(I sent this one to Miami Beach, where she was on vacation.)

*May 9, 1952*

*Dearest Colleen,*

*Hi love. Sorry I haven't written long before this and while I'm at it, I better say I'm double sorry because we go into the woods tomorrow and seeing as we have to walk six miles carrying food and all, I won't be coming out each day to mail a letter. So this short note will let you know that I received your two wonderful letters which I was very happy to receive as I too have missed you more than you'll know.*

*. . . Well love it's getting on and we're due out of here at 4:30 in the morning. So I'll leave you with the thought in your mind that there's a fisherman up north who is missing you like crazy.*

*As ever,*
*Love and all, Gord*

*June 14, 1952*

*Hi dear,*

*Once again I have heard three sweet words from you which I should use more often and that is, "I miss you." They sound awful good to me coming from such a sweet young lady as you and again I say I should use them much more often. But the truth is I don't know too much of sweet words so just give me time as I am a comer.*

*Love, Gordie*

*June 16, 1952*

*Hello dear,*

*Guess what—little Gord received not one but two very nice letters from you today which is setting a pace I really can't hold up to, but believe me it is awful nice.*

*It sounds like you're having yourself one wonderful time this summer which is very nice. I only wish I were there with you to enjoy your company and to see all the nice places and also to enjoy the sun as it's something we haven't seen out here for the last week.*

*Love, Gordon*

*June 28, 1952*

*I sure wish you weren't so darn far away so I could run down to see you on weekends. But as it is, it takes me a week's driving to get there and back. It would be nice if you also lived right here. Seeing as I'm dreaming, I might as well go all out. As it is, I'll just have to go on missing you until I get the call from Adams.*

*And also, I don't know as yet just where I'll be staying in Detroit because, as I said before, Adams would like to see me back with Ma Shaw and the boys.*

*Well dear, it's needless to say that I miss you. Of course there's joy in hearing from you all the time, but it's not like the real thing as you well know.*

*As always, Love, Gord*

*July 3, 1952*

*Dear Colleen,*

*First on order is the thought of the day. "Love me or leave me, or let me be lonely, my love is your love to share with you only, I'd rather be lonely than happy with somebody new." This song just finished playing so I thought it a good way to let someone know they have been missed by a farm boy.*

*Love, Gordie*

*July 23, 1952*

*Dear Colleen,*

*Hello dear. Well at long last they sent me home from the lake long enough to have a little party for my brother Vern and his family, and so I could get a letter off to you to let you know all is well and that I miss you and enjoy your letters very much.*

*Love, Gordon*

Colleen said the moment she knew we belonged together happened when I came back to Detroit that fall. She heard my voice on the phone and realized I was the one for her. As for me, I knew it from the first time we talked at the bowling alley. As the next off-season approached, I was sure I didn't want to spend another summer apart. I asked her to come to Canada with me, but she refused. It wouldn't be proper, she said, to go all that way to meet my parents as things stood. I agreed.

By that point I knew everything I needed to about Colleen Joffa. I got down on one knee and asked her to marry me. We'd dated for long enough that we decided to skip a formal engagement. On April 15, 1953, we headed over to Calvary Presbyterian, a big old brick church on Grand River Avenue in Detroit. Like so many buildings in Detroit, it's fallen on hard times now, which is tough to see. Back then, though, it was exactly the type of church you picture when you imagine a wedding. The sun was shining through the stained-glass windows when Colleen appeared in the doorway at the back of the church. I know that every groom says this, but she was the prettiest bride you ever saw. Pat Lindsay was her maid of honor, while Ted Lindsay, Marty Pavelich, and Reggie Sinclair were there to stand up for me. Any player lucky enough to win the Stanley Cup will tell you it's the best feeling you can have on the ice. I treasure each one of our championships, but I can say without a flicker of hesitation that the five happiest days of my life were when Colleen agreed to become Mrs. Gordie Howe and when our four children were born.

*Six*

# THE GLORY YEARS

T he Detroit Red Wings, as they're now known, took shape in 1932 when James Norris rode into town with a hat full of cash to save the city's struggling NHL franchise. The team's first incarnation joined the league in 1926 as the Detroit Cougars. Its foundation came all the way from Vancouver Island, after the Victoria club was forced to find a new home when the Western Hockey League dissolved. A naming contest was held for fans a few years later and the team was rechristened the Detroit Falcons. However, a new name didn't exactly inspire the Falcons to soar to greater heights. To put a winner on the ice the club needed cash, something its owners were either unable or unwilling to pony up. The Falcons fell into receivership and needed a new owner who was willing to run the team on more than a shoestring budget. It found its meal ticket in the deep-pocketed Mr. Norris, who had made a fortune in grain, cattle, and shipping. He'd dreamed of owning an NHL franchise for years, but couldn't make it happen in Chicago, where his empire was based. He'd kept a close eye on the fortunes of the struggling Detroit franchise and when an opening came up, he pounced. In his younger days, Mr. Norris played for the Winged Wheelers of the Montreal Amateur Athletic Association, and the game of hockey had stayed in his blood. When the Red Wings debuted in the 1932–33 season, the team had a new owner, a new name, and a new logo, a wheel with wings inspired by the owner's old amateur club—and a nod to Detroit's stature as the Motor City.

The change in ownership still didn't mean that Detroit would be putting a winner on the ice. No one knew that better than the team's coach and general manager. A former professional player, Jack Adams had been with the Detroit organization since 1927, its second year in the league. By the time he met Mr. Norris in 1932, he had little to show for his time with the club. Regardless, I guess Mr. Norris still liked what he saw, because he offered Mr. Adams a one-year deal. If Mr. Adams could make good, he'd get another shot at it the next year. And that's exactly what happened.

Looser purse strings brought better players to the team and the one-year trial period between owner and coach, sealed with a handshake, was extended for another season. Another followed, and then another. In 1936, Detroit broke through with its first Stanley Cup. In 1937, it won again. The Norris–Adams partnership was off and rolling. It continued for thirty years, all of them without a formal contract. It's hard to imagine an understanding like that coming to pass in today's NHL, where coaches are routinely locked into multiyear deals worth millions of dollars. In any case, by the time I came along, the Red Wings had added a third Stanley Cup in 1943.

Coming up in the league, the young Jack Adams was known for playing a tough brand of hockey. His philosophy didn't change when he moved behind the bench. When Tommy Ivan became coach I remember him echoing Mr. Adams's belief that hockey was a simple game with only two basic maneuvers: either you knock the puck away from the man or you knock the man away from the puck. Both men believed in playing hard-checking two-way hockey. As an extension of that doctrine, the organization looked for players who tried equally hard in both directions. If you didn't back-check as a forward or a center, you weren't long for the Red Wings; it was as simple as that.

When it came to constructing his hockey club, Trader Jack wasn't one to shy away from pulling the trigger on a big deal, no matter how much it shook up the team. For better or worse, it was actually part of his philosophy of team building. After one of Detroit's Stanley Cup wins in the 1930s he stood pat, only to watch the Wings, in his mind, become less hungry the following season. He told himself it was the last time he would be complacent. From then on, regardless of how well his team did the year before, he remained unsentimental about his players. Anyone could be traded. It's been said that I was an exception to this rule, but I'm not sure that's exactly right. It's probably true that our relationship—Mr. Adams called me the "Big Guy" in a way that might pass for affection if you squinted hard—was better than the ones he had with most of his players, but it's not like I couldn't have been traded. I knew that my spot on the team depended on how I performed on the ice and little else. I felt like it wasn't good business to get too confident about my place in the league. Starting out, I constantly worried about being demoted to the minors and, even when I became more established, I still felt like I was playing for my job every time I stepped on the ice. It's an attitude that was likely passed down from my father. Growing up, he told us we shouldn't ever get too comfortable with what we had, because something could always come along to take it away.

After winning a championship, most general managers are willing to give their players a chance to defend the title. Not Jack Adams. He wouldn't sit still, even after we won our first Stanley Cup together in 1950 (the year I was out with the concussion). In the off-season he engineered one of the biggest trades in league history. Typically, a goalie who just won the Stanley Cup is treated like he's worth his weight in gold, but that's not how it went for Harry Lumley, who was shipped out the door to the Black Hawks. Joining Harry in Chicago were Black Jack Stewart, an All-Star defenseman, as well as Don Morrison, Al Dewsbury, and Pete Babando, who'd just won the Cup for us with his overtime heroics. In return, we got Metro Prystai, Gaye Stewart, and goalie Jim Henry. We were stunned when the news broke. Seeing Metro in red and white would be good, but losing so many of our teammates was tough to swallow. The press was equally shocked and our fans didn't seem to know how to feel about the trade either. As it turned out, Mr. Adams had a larger plan. He was clearing the way for a young goalie named Terry Sawchuk, who had played a few games for us the year before. Mr. Adams felt that Lumley's days as a top-flight goalie were numbered and that Sawchuk was ready to take over. As the years went on, Sawchuk proved to be one of the best to ever put on pads, so making room for him in the lineup worked out in retrospect. At the time, though, seeing Lumley moved to the Black Hawks with little more than a nod didn't make us feel very warm inside. As much as I loved playing hockey, it was moments like those that reinforced the business side of the sport. Someone else was always signing your paychecks, and as long as they kept coming you had little alternative but to say good-bye to your friends and get to know your new teammates. Whether you liked it or not, when the puck dropped you still had a job to do.

In 1950–51, our job was to defend our Stanley Cup championship. That was the plan anyway, but when we reached the playoffs that season, Montreal had its own ideas. Some people tried to blame our flameout that year on the big off-season shake-up, but I don't think the argument holds much water. Sure, we missed Lumley, Stewart, and the rest, but the 101 points we put up in the regular season suggest that chemistry wasn't a problem. I'm not about to make any excuses for our team. Montreal won and they deserve the credit for beating us. From the Rocket on down, they were tough in that series. It just goes to show how little the oddsmakers really know about anything. They had us as favorites going in, but nobody ever wins anything on paper. Once we got on the ice, we didn't deliver. The next season, we knew, would have to be different.

For my money, the 1951–52 edition of the Red Wings was the best team we ever had in Detroit. Mr. Adams had another busy off-season. He brought in Tony Leswick through a trade with the Rangers and Black Hawks. He also sold six more players to Chicago for $75,000 in cash: Clare Martin, George Gee, Jim McFadden, Jimmy Peters, Clare Raglan, and Max McNab. The open roster spots allowed us to bring in Glen Skov, Johnny Wilson, Marty Pavelich, Benny Woit, and Alex Delvecchio. We had Vic Stasiuk and Bob Goldham already from the previous year. The new blood meshed with the veterans right away. Ted, Sid, and I were still going strong as the Production Line. Metro was settling in nicely in his second year with the team. Our blue line was rock solid, anchored by Red Kelly, Marcel Pronovost, and Leo Reise Jr. In net, we had Sawchuk, who won the Vezina Trophy that year as the league's best goalie. We could score, we could skate, we could check, and we were even a little bit mean. In short, we were stacked. Seeing that much talent in one place when I went to work every day was a pleasure.

At only nineteen, Delvecchio took over as the baby of the team. You wouldn't have known it by the way he handled the puck, though. He was magic. In his first year with the club, Alex centered Metro Prystai and Johnny Wilson on the third line. The second line featured Skov at center with Pavelich and Leswick on the wings. In previous seasons, the Red Wings had leaned heavily on the Production Line to handle most of the scoring. We didn't mind, but on nights when we didn't have it going, the team could struggle to get on the board. All that changed in 1951. Our squad had three full lines that scored as well as they checked. Add in Red Kelly, who might have been the best offensive defenseman the NHL had seen until Bobby Orr came along, and we had as much firepower as you could ever want.

With all of that talent on hand, we ripped through the league again that year. For the second season in a row we cracked the century mark, tallying 100 points even. With 44 wins against only 14 losses and 12 ties, we were 22 points clear of Montreal, which finished in second place. By the time the playoffs came around, we couldn't have been more ready to make up for the previous year. The semifinals against Toronto started like a dream. Sawchuk posted back-to-back shutouts and we cruised to a quick 2–0 series lead. The Leafs finally solved the puzzle in game three with a pair of goals. Fortunately, we were there to pick up our goalie, lighting the lamp six times for a relatively easy 6–2 win. Three wins in a row wasn't enough to calm down Mr. Adams, who wouldn't stop being nervous until the final horn sounded. Between games he kept saying that no lead was ever safe. He reminded us that in 1942 we were up 3–0 on the Leafs, only to lose the series. This edition of the Red Wings wasn't about to make the same mistake. We closed the door with a 3–1 victory and a series sweep. After losing so many big games to Toronto early in my career, it was satisfying to lay down such a sound beating. At that moment, the league felt as if it was undergoing a changing of the guard. The Leafs were still the defending champions, but the signs pointed to an end to their dynasty. Their best players were getting long in the tooth, while we were young and coming on strong. We liked our chances not just for that year, but also for years to come. I'm sure the Habs, who were also young and hungry, felt the same way.

While we were rolling into the Stanley Cup finals in four games, the Canadiens and the Bruins were locked in a war in the other semifinal. The Rocket finally put Montreal over the top in game seven. Earlier in the game, he'd been knocked unconscious after being upended by Leo Labine. Say what you will about the Rocket, but he was a tough customer. He had to be helped off the ice and took some stitches to fix a cut over his eye, but late in the third period with the score tied 1–1, he reentered the game. No medical staff today would have let him sit on the bench, let alone get back on the ice, but that was a different era. With time running down, he collected the puck deep in his own zone, skated the length of the ice through the defense, cut to the front of the net, and made a move to beat Sugar Jim Henry for the game-winner. I wasn't there, but I was told that the Forum erupted with one of the loudest roars you'll ever hear. Habs fans count it as maybe the greatest of the Rocket's 544 career goals and 82 playoff goals.

The victory earned the Canadiens the right to face us for the Stanley Cup. We couldn't wait. By taking care of the Leafs in short order, we'd given our bumps and bruises time to heal. The Habs, on the other hand, were pretty banged up. However, just as I won't make any excuses for us losing the year before, I won't make any for them either. (Nor, I'm sure, would they ask me to.) The series opened with a first game that's best remembered for how strangely it ended. Late in the third period we were up 2–1 when the Forum announcer signaled the last minute of play. Montreal's coach, Dick Irvin, pulled his goalie, but the extra attacker didn't help and Lindsay scored on the empty net to make it 3–1. After the goal, the Forum announcer told the building that another minute of play remained. Irvin was furious. He claimed that the timekeeper's mistake led to the empty-net goal. It didn't matter, though. No coach's tantrum was going to change the final score. We followed up the win with another in Montreal and returned to the friendly confines of the Olympia with a two-game lead in the series. In game three we came through with a 3–0 shutout victory to put us one game away from the Cup. As it turned out, four games were all it took. In the season's final game, Sawchuk delivered another shutout, backstopping us to a 3–0 win. Technically, it was my second Stanley Cup, but in my heart it's the first one I feel like I had a hand in winning. When we won it all in 1950, I was in street clothes watching from the stands. This time I was out there sweating and bleeding with the boys. It was beautiful.

Our back-to-back sweeps made us the first team to ever go undefeated through both playoff rounds to win the Stanley Cup. As good as we were offensively, our defense was even better. As a team, we allowed only 5 goals in eight games and Sawchuk, who had four shutouts in the playoffs, didn't allow a single goal on home ice. Naturally, we didn't spend an extra second feeling bad for Montreal. Not that they needed us to. As any Habs fan can tell you, they'd be back—plenty. The Canadiens have had their share of playoff heartaches, but that's only because they were good enough to put themselves in a position to be disappointed in the first place. Between 1951 and 1960, they made it to the Stanley Cup finals ten years in a row. They won six times over those years, including five straight Cups to end the decade. As good as they would become, though, the first half of the 1950s belonged to us. It's not my way to be cocky, but if the playoffs had lasted another couple of months, I feel like the team we had in 1952 could have played for the rest of the summer and still not lost a game. The way we clamped down on our opponents led some to say that we strangled them. As it turned out, a local fish vendor really took that phrase to heart. In the final game of the series, he packed an octopus with him and threw it on the ice at the Olympia as a strange symbol of how we treated the competition. Detroit fans have kept the tradition alive for more than sixty years.

Younger sports fans won't remember the days of the player–coach, but for many years it wasn't that unusual to see a coach also suit up as a player. Nowadays, the demands of professional sports wouldn't leave enough time in the day to handle both jobs. The game planning and play calling, not to mention dealing with the media, has become more complex and time consuming. In the old days, though, paying one salary for two jobs was a way for a cash-strapped team to save money. Some of the more notable player–coaches include Bill Russell, who did both jobs for the Boston Celtics after Red Auerbach retired; Pete Rose in the 1980s with the Cincinnati Reds; and Frank Robinson at the end of his playing career with the Cleveland Indians. In 1952, Sid Abel joined that list, but it wasn't with the Red Wings. In the off-season after our Stanley Cup victory, Sid agreed to become the player–coach of the Chicago Black Hawks. They were perennially scuffling around near the bottom of the standings and the league wanted to see weaker teams become more competitive. With that in mind, Mr. Adams arranged a trade that made Sid a Black Hawk. It was a deal that marked the end of the original Production Line.

With Sid in Chicago, Alex Delvecchio took over as the first-line center. Much like Sid, he had a sixth sense that allowed him to deliver the puck to where you were going, not where you had just been. Like Ted, he grew up in northern Ontario. He was from Fort William, a town at the tip of Lake Superior that eventually became Thunder Bay. Like me, his time in the junior ranks didn't last long. He was in Oshawa for a year playing for the Generals and then spent only six games in Indianapolis before being called up to the big club. Most Detroit fans probably remember Alex as a grizzled veteran of dozens of NHL campaigns. By the time he retired, he'd racked up enough seasons to count among the club's all-time leaders in games played. That's not how I remember him, though. I can still see him as a baby-faced rookie. Young or not, he was good enough to convince Mr. Adams that Sid was expendable. It was no small feat. Sid wasn't that far removed from winning the Hart Trophy and he remained a large piece of the team's heart and soul. He taught a lot of young players, including me, how to handle ourselves both on and off the ice. For Trader Jack, though, such softer considerations didn't often register in his way of thinking. All he saw was a young player on the way up and one who might be past his best days. It didn't matter to him that we had just won the Cup a few months earlier. He was already looking ahead to the next season.

When it came to the Red Wings, the roster wasn't the only thing Mr. Adams wanted to micromanage. No matter how big or small the matter, he had an opinion. Oftentimes he'd even venture into areas that any reasonable person would consider off-limits. On the road, he wanted us to behave like gentlemen. Shirts and ties were mandatory and he even wanted to be sure that we tipped properly. That was fine. His objections to drinking and smoking were also understandable. Less appropriate were his opinions on the opposite sex. If he'd had his way, players would have remained celibate for the entire hockey season. This extended even to married couples. Fooling around at home, he reasoned, diminished a player's drive on the ice. I can't say we paid him much heed on that one. As young as we were, we could still recognize what was in bounds and what was a bridge too far. That being said, many of us did respect his dictum about getting married in-season. He considered it a distraction and wanted wedding dates scheduled for the off-season. Even Ted, who wasn't one to abide by other people's rules, adhered to that one and waited until the season ended to marry Pat.

It's hard to imagine a club's general manager these days having anywhere near the power that Mr. Adams wielded back then. For someone who wanted to rule with an iron fist, though, the circumstances were nearly ideal. In the postwar years, the competition for jobs was fierce. Players who might otherwise never have risen out of the junior ranks were promoted to the big leagues to fill the spots vacated by players who left to serve in the military. When they returned, those veterans found that their replacements had developed into bona fide NHL players. A glut of quality talent chasing a finite number of jobs gave teams a lot of power.

For someone who wasn't afraid to use it, like Mr. Adams, it was a perfect storm. With jobs at such a premium, you really had to watch your step when he was around. If you got on the wrong side of the boss, Lord only knows where you might have ended up. And he had a lot of bad sides.

Training camp was a time when Mr. Adams always seemed to be around. You had to keep your guard up, because you didn't know when he might appear. After practice, a few of us would sometimes unwind by playing golf. When we'd finished, we might stop in at the clubhouse for a few beers. Sharing a post-round drink on the deck with your friends seems innocent enough, but when you played for Jack Adams, innocence was always in the eye of the beholder. On those days, I'd always be nervous about running into him with beer on my breath. We all were. It was a surefire way to get into his bad books. We were grown men, but sometimes it felt like we were kids sneaking around our parents. Wherever we stayed, I spent a lot of extra time taking the scenic route home to make sure I didn't run into him.

One year, around 1954 or so, Colleen and I threw a party for the team at our house. Just to be proper, Colleen thought it would be best to invite the club's brass. When we asked Tommy Ivan to attend, he said thanks but no thanks. In his mind, a team party wasn't the right place for a coach. He did suggest that we invite Jack and Helen Adams, though. They definitely wouldn't attend, he said, but it would be a nice gesture. Wouldn't you know it: Not only did the old bugger show up, but he was the first person through the door. He also acted like the life of the party. He posed for pictures with all of the wives and generally had himself a pretty big time. As for the rest of us, having our teetotaler boss around kind of put a damper on things. I'd picked up a bunch of beer for the guys, but we had to keep it under wraps. Just imagine how strange it would feel to hide booze at your own party in your own house. I stashed it in the basement in some laundry tubs filled with ice. When guys arrived, I'd quietly tell them that what they were looking for was in the basement. All night long, guys were slipping off downstairs to have a beer, because none of us dared to drink in front of the boss.

In Detroit, you could never be too sure how much Mr. Adams knew about what you were up to. He maintained a network of informants—which probably included Ma Shaw—to keep an eye on his players. I was pretty lucky in that regard. When it comes to booze, I'm not much of a drinker. A couple of beers in an evening are pretty much my maximum. Some of my teammates, on the other hand, would spill more in a night than I drank. They always tried to be smart about it, though. When they were out on the town, they didn't often linger in one spot for more than a drink or two before moving to another location. They never wanted it reported to Mr. Adams that his players were out drinking all night long. Moving around allowed them to maintain some plausible deniability.

Despite the strategies we used to thwart his meddling, somehow the old coot was still able to keep an eye on darn near everything. He even knew what I was up to in the off-season. After hockey and fishing, my next great sporting love was baseball. Ever since I was a kid, every spring when hockey season ended I'd put away my skates and get out my ball glove. Even after I made the NHL, I'd still go back to Saskatoon in the summers to play baseball. At the time, there were several good semi-pro leagues throughout western Canada. I played for Saskatoon in the Northern Saskatchewan Baseball League. We went up against teams from towns like North Battleford, Prince Albert, and Delisle. Sometimes I'd also travel with other teams to play in cash tournaments. In my early days in the NHL, I could make almost as much money playing baseball as I earned from hockey.

One year, I remember playing in a tournament in Indian Head, which is just east of Regina. The caliber of baseball was pretty good, especially for a small town in the middle of the Prairies. The tournament even attracted an All-Star team from the Negro leagues that made the trip up to Canada to play. A scout for the New York Yankees—I think his name was Roy Taylor—was also there watching. I was seeing the ball well that weekend and in one game I even hit for the cycle, which means a single, a double, a triple, and a home run. Overall, I went 8 for 11, and I think the Yankees were looking at me as a potential prospect. Their interest quickly faded once they found out I was already playing professional hockey, but I was still flattered for the look. I don't know if I would have had the goods to make it to the big leagues, but it's not like I spent much time over the years thinking about what-ifs. Hockey was so good to me I don't have much room to harbor regrets about another sport. Suffice to say that baseball's a wonderful game. I loved playing it right up until the day Mr. Adams put a stop to it.

In the summer of 1952, I was playing in a tournament in Regina when I received a telegram from Mr. Adams that read, "Who's going to pay your bills if you get hurt? I suggest you quit playing." It was a tough note to get. I didn't want to entertain the thought of hanging up my cleats. At the same time, hockey was my livelihood and Mr. Adams was my boss, so I felt stuck. I had to respond, but I knew that once I did, my days on the diamond would be numbered. There was a tournament coming up in Kamsack, which is east of Saskatoon, that I wanted to play in, so I waited before getting back to Mr. Adams. I figured that, at the very least, some stalling could buy me a few more games. When I finally replied, my telegram

*The only thing better than playing hockey for a living is playing hockey for a living with your sons. Though I loved Detroit, playing with Marty and Mark in Houston (above) completely restored my love of the game, even though I had retired shortly before. Our move to New England eventually brought about something none of us expected: a return to the NHL. Here we are, years later, with our old Whalers sweaters at the WHA Hall of Fame booth.*

*It doesn't matter how much gray hair you have, you never lose your love of the game. I never missed a chance to get back on the ice, and you can tell by the smiles that I enjoyed it. Here I am at the 1999 All-Star Game in Tampa. One thing the greatest players have in common is that they love the game. I don't think many people love it more than Bobby Orr (below).*

There is nothing more important than friends and family. That's Colleen sharing a laugh with close family friend Al Philpot on his boat in Miami. Here we all are at Colleen's 65th birthday party: Cathy, Mark, my older brother Vern, Colleen, Murray, Marty, and me. I have gone from being the kid in the family to the great-grandfather. Here I am holding Travis and Kristen's daughter Ainsley.

*One of the great things about our game is the people you meet and the tradition you become part of. Here I am at the Order of Hockey in Canada inaugural ceremony with the great Wayne Gretzky, the guy who broke so many of my records, Olympian Cassie Campbell, and Hall of Famer Frank Mahovlich. Below that I'm at Joe Carter's charity golf tournament with Eddie Shack, Marty, and Johnny Bower. And the bottom photo shows me with some of the greatest Red Wings ever: my former linemate Ted Lindsay, former captain Steve Yzerman, and legendary coach Scotty Bowman, at Steve's retirement.*

As much as I love the game, life has been great in retirement. Here I am accepting an honorary degree from University of Saskatchewan. And below that is Mark at his Hall of Fame induction in 2011. I could not have been more proud. And the bottom photo was taken at Marty's, where I still like to get out and do yard work.

Hockey is about tradition and teamwork, and I am
very proud to have become part of both in Detroit.
Here I am as the Stanley Cup was presented in 1955.
From left to right, that's Marguerite Norris, Vic
Stasiuk, Clarence Campbell, Ted Lindsay, Marcel
Bonin (with his hand on the Cup), Bill Dineen
(directly behind Bonin), Jimmy Skinner, Glen Skov
(behind Skinner), Alex Delvecchio (with his hand on
Wilson's shoulder), Johnny Wilson (directly behind
me), me, and Terry Sawchuk. At the right is a photo
of me signing a whole bunch of number 9 sweaters,
and below that is a photo of the Wings all wearing
my old number in 2013 to mark my 85th birthday.

*I first met Bobby when he was a kid, and played against him in his first NHL game. Years later, we're still friends. Here I am with him and Marty taking in a Panthers game.*

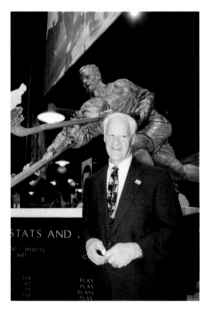

*As a kid growing up in Saskatchewan, I never dreamed I'd have a statue with my name on it. What an incredible honor.*

*I never did get to play in the Olympics, but I did get to carry the torch for the 2010 Winter Games in Vancouver. It was special to be part of that.*

*I will always think of hockey as an outdoor sport, since that is the way I first played it. That's just one more reason I enjoyed dropping the puck for Steve Yzerman and Darryl Sittler at the alumni game at the Winter Classic in 2014. But really, it doesn't matter where the ice is—the game will never change.*

said, "Dear Jack Adams, are you serious?" I figured it would take him a while to track me down, but unfortunately that's not how it played out. When his return telegram found me in Kamsack, it read simply, "I am serious." Those three little words pretty much ended my semi-pro baseball career.

I might have played longer if not for an injury that drew some attention earlier in the summer. I was playing third base when I fielded a double-play ball, stepped on the bag, and fired it over to first for the out. As I made the play, the other team's first baseman was charging in from second. Trying to break up the throw, he came in cleats up and spiked me. He probably learned it from watching Ty Cobb. His cleats broke through my skin and I ended up with blood poisoning. When the news reached Mr. Adams, that was all it took for him to snap into action. The really annoying part of the whole thing was how far the guy had to run off the base path to get me. By the time I finished my throw to first, I was about six feet off the bag. I wouldn't go so far as to say I'm vindictive, but it was a dirty slide and I felt like there was a score that needed to be settled. In my next three at-bats I drag bunted each time until I flipped the script on him. It took three tries, but I finally put one squarely down the first base line. He charged in to field the ball and I ran straight up his leg with my cleats. Later, he told me that he should have just stood there and let me hit him the first time, because I was going to get him sooner or later. He was right about that. Tit for tat, I say.

I still shake my head when I think about how Jack Adams was able to take baseball away from me with nothing more than a simple telegram. But that's how much control he had over his team. It chafed us, but there wasn't much to be done about it. Whether he was the coach or general manager, he maintained something of a love–hate relationship with his players. It would be hard to find a more frustrating boss. One minute he'd praise a guy for his effort, and the next he'd bench him for unknown reasons. He could be moody and unpredictable, and when he was angry he'd lash out at whoever was closest. Worst of all, he tried to exercise an unacceptable measure of control over the lives of his players. That's what bothered me the most. On a professional level, some of his moves still baffle me to this day. Sometimes he would cut bait on a player he thought was past his prime, only to see that same guy return to torture us for years to come. That's certainly what happened with Red Kelly, to name just one example. It didn't matter to Mr. Adams, though. If he found even a hint of something he didn't like, you were out the door.

To be fair, Mr. Adams did have his redeeming qualities, particularly when he was away from the arena. He had a strong work ethic and he tried to pass that along to his players. I credit him with instilling in me some of the discipline that helped me to succeed as a professional athlete. He was also the person who gave me a shot at the big leagues, which is something I'll always appreciate. The press would occasionally speculate about how much I grew to dislike Mr. Adams over the years. We weren't best friends, but then again that's not really the relationship you need to have with your boss. If I were to try to encapsulate my feelings in a nutshell, I guess I'd say that I might have hated some of his actions, but I never hated him as a person.

Longtime Red Wings fans have their own opinions on Jack Adams. On the plus side of the ledger, he gets a lot of credit for being the architect of our championship teams in the early 1950s. To be fair, it should be noted that he didn't do it alone. Detroit's chief scout, Carson Cooper, for one, could pick a needle out of a haystack when it came to evaluating hockey talent. The criticisms of Trader Jack can be traced back to his propensity to make big roster moves at the expense of chemistry. They say it's one of the reasons his teams didn't often win back-to-back Stanley Cups. Personally, I don't know if it's that straightforward. Winning a championship in any sport isn't exactly a cakewalk. It's not like the other good teams in the league are ever going to just roll over. Toss in a few unlucky injuries and a bad bounce here or there and nothing is ever guaranteed. For the Red Wings, 1953 was one of those years.

Once again, we finished on top of the league, 15 points clear of the second-place Canadiens. We were also 21 points better than Boston, whom we were slotted to face in the semifinals of the playoffs. We had owned them in our head-to-head matchups during the regular season and were feeling confident going into the series. Boy, were we in for a surprise. The Bruins beat us in six games and, just like that, our season was over. As the defending Stanley Cup champions, to fall flat against a team we thought we thoroughly outclassed was obviously a big letdown. That season, it wasn't my only disappointment.

If I had to choose my favorite thing in hockey, it would be assisting on a goal. Don't get me wrong: I enjoyed putting the puck in the net, but making a great pass strikes a different type of chord. It's like distilling what it means to be part of a team into a single action. When you help a teammate to score, he wins, you win, and so does the club. It's like hitting the trifecta. As much as I always looked to make the best hockey play, at the end of the 1952–53 season my teammates were less interested in being set up and more concerned with helping me to score. I was having a great year shooting the puck. Every time I got a clean look, it seemed like the puck found its way into the back of the net. In the third to last game of the season, I scored twice against Boston to put my tally at 49. I was 1 goal shy of the record set by the Rocket in 1945, with two games remaining. Everyone in the NHL knew that the Rocket took a lot of pride in that record, as well as in his status as the league's top goal scorer. For the most part, I didn't give too much thought to that sort of thing. I figured that if I played well, the team would win and everything else would fall into place. Given the rivalry between the Wings and the Canadiens, though, it would be a lie to say I didn't want to break the Rocket's record once I got close. We didn't like the Habs and they didn't like us. Taking away the Rocket's record would have been a satisfying way to poke a stick in their eye. For his part, Jack Adams badly wanted to see it happen, as did Tommy Ivan and my teammates. In our penultimate game of the season, against the Black Hawks, Tommy gave me some extra shifts, but I came up empty. With one game left in the regular season, I remained stuck at 49 goals.

Our final game, at home against the Canadiens, had all of the elements needed to be fairly poetic. The press went into overdrive talking about the possibility of me breaking the record while skating against the Rocket himself. It was a nice thought, but when the puck dropped the game didn't work out that way. Once again, Tommy had me on the ice for some extra shifts, but every time I jumped over the boards I found Montreal left winger Bert Olmstead attached to my hip like some sort of pesky shadow. I found out later that Dick Irvin told him to stick to me like glue. I think Irvin cared more about stopping me that night than he did about winning the game. At one point, I was at our net talking to Sawchuk during a break in the action, and Olmstead was right there with us. I asked him what he was doing, but he didn't say a word. I almost have to admire him for following his coach's instructions to the letter. Even with Olmstead stalking me, I had a few chances on Gerry McNeil that night, but didn't manage to put one by him. Irvin was overjoyed and, true to form, pretty obnoxious about his boys shutting me down that night. He slid across the ice and raised the Rocket's arm as if he were still the heavyweight champion of the world. As it turned out, 49 goals ended up being the high-water mark in my career. Along with my 46 assists, I finished the season with 95 points, which was the highest total anyone had ever put up at that point. The funny thing is, I think I did get that 50th goal. In February we had a game in Boston. Late in the third period, Red Kelly fired a shot from the blue line that got past goalkeeper Jim Henry. I was pretty sure I tipped that shot in, and a lot of my teammates agreed, but the officials didn't see it. At the time, I wasn't as close to the 50 goal mark, so I wasn't too concerned. But looking back, it would have been nice if that one had counted.

Some people, including Irvin, suggested that the reason we lost to Boston in the playoffs that year was because I was too tired from chasing the Rocket's record during the regular season. I don't really buy into that line of thinking. I might have taken a few more shifts, but for the most part I was just playing hockey as usual. I was still only twenty-five years old at that point, and my body recovered pretty quickly. Physically, I don't remember running out of steam against the Bruins. Mentally, I can't say that I recall the pressure being too hard to handle either. The chase for 50 goals that season certainly wasn't anything compared to the pressure I felt in 1963 when I was closing in on the Rocket's career total of 544. That was definitely more of a grind. Sometimes there's just no convenient explanation for why teams lose. I still think we had a great squad in 1953. Rather than trying to figure out why we lost, credit should really go to Boston for beating us. Unfortunately for the Bruins, they couldn't keep it going in the next round. They ended up losing to the Canadiens in five games. It was Montreal's third straight appearance in the finals, but their first Stanley Cup since 1946. We knew they'd be tough to beat in the following season. Then again, we knew we would be, too.

*Seven*

# MY MOST
# IMPORTANT TEAM

Growing up, if hockey wasn't my sole focus at any given time, it was close. It was a way of life for me from as far back as I can remember. As I kid, I can recall sitting at the kitchen table and writing out different signatures to try to figure out the best one to use once I became famous. When I finished, I tugged on the hem of my mom's skirt and asked her to pick a favorite. She humored me and chose one with big loops on the "G" and the "H." To this day, it's the one I still use whenever I sign my name. Even as a fanciful child, though, I wasn't interested in the perks of fame. I just figured that if I was going to play hockey for a living, I'd need a serviceable autograph. At sixteen, when the Red Wings wanted me to move to Galt to play on the practice squad, I said yes because I knew it would make me a better hockey player. I didn't particularly want to leave my friends and family in Saskatoon, but when hockey called, I always listened. For more than twenty years I was content to let hockey guide nearly all of my decisions. It was that way right up until the moment I met Colleen.

At some point, I suppose it happens to most everyone. Or at least it does if you're lucky. You're ticking along worrying only about yourself until one day you wake up and something's different. One minute it was just you, and then suddenly all of your decisions are being made for two. The funny thing is how seamlessly this change comes about. Once I met Colleen, everything just sort of clicked into place. I'll tell anyone who will listen that marrying her was the smartest thing I ever did. I wouldn't say that hockey took a back seat to our marriage—that would be Jack Adams talking—but for the first time in my life I wanted to make room for something besides the game. As if that wasn't enough, not long after we were hitched, Colleen and I had to start thinking for three. Our first child, Marty, was born on February 18, 1954. We named him after Marty Pavelich. There was no way to know it beforehand, but once Marty came along I realized I was born to be a family man. I'd guess that fathers from the beginning of time have been saying the same thing. Of course, most fathers don't have a boss like Jack Adams. Trying to raise a family on his watch was easier said than done.

As much as I wanted to be there when our son was born, babies don't care about clocks, calendars, or hockey schedules. The night Marty arrived, the Red Wings were on the road in Montreal. A bunch of smiling teammates gave me the news between periods. I gladly accepted the handshakes and "attaboys," knowing full well that Colleen had done all of the heavy lifting. Unfortunately, the Canadiens didn't feel like cooperating with what was other-wise a banner night for the Howe family. The headline in the next morning's paper read: HOWES HAVE BABY; RED WINGS LOSE. I didn't mind it so much, but Colleen thought the story implied that we'd lost because I was more focused on our baby than the game. Jack Adams, true to form, did his part to worsen her mood. The day Colleen and Marty were set to be released from the hospital coincided with the end of our road trip. I couldn't wait to kiss my wife and meet my new baby boy, but unbeknownst to us, Mr. Adams had his own backward ideas. He called our doctor, Jim Matthews, and asked if Colleen could be kept in the hospital for one more day. Mr. Adams was afraid my mind wouldn't be on that night's game if Colleen and the baby came home. Jim, of course, was a doctor not a hockey player, and he had no problem telling Mr. Adams to go to hell. Still, the full Jack Adams experience wasn't lost on Colleen.

The team's attitude toward wives never sat well with Colleen, and quite rightly so. Mr. Adams wanted a player's mind to be on hockey, full stop. Wives were to be kept separate, just like a player's religious beliefs. The club assumed that players had them, but they didn't want to know about it. Mr. Adams didn't want us to have any outside interests—family, business, or otherwise—that would distract us from the game. It was a ridiculous stance, but he took it seriously. What's more, he even tried to regulate our sex lives. Given his way, players would have sex only in the off-season. He'd routinely come into the locker room and tell us to keep it in our pants. In his mind, having sex was like losing a pint of blood. It hurt your stamina on the ice and took away the jump in your legs. After one loss, I remember him getting so angry that he told a young newlywed that his play was suffering because he was spending too much time in the crease at home. That one had us cracking up behind our gloves, but Mr. Adams was dead serious. As I said, he could be a ridiculous man. It's hard to imagine a coach trying to get away with anything close to that now, but this was the 1950s and that was Jack Adams.

The 1953–54 season was one of the rare times when Mr. Adams resisted the urge to make any major changes to the roster. He did make a few tweaks, however, most notably reaching down to the farm system and promoting Earl "Dutch" Reibel. With Dutch in the fold, Tommy Ivan decided to shift him into Alex Delvecchio's spot on the Production Line, putting Alex between Metro Prystai and Johnny Wilson. The move seemed to work. We finished on top of the standings for a sixth consecutive year, with 88 points. Montreal racked up 81, which was good for second place, followed by Toronto with 78. In his second year behind the bench for the hapless Black Hawks, poor Sid Abel finished in the cellar with only 12 wins and 31 points. Along with the Canadiens, we were clearly the class of the league. Between our two teams, we had the top seven point getters in the NHL. I claimed the Art Ross Trophy with 81 points, 14 clear of the Rocket, while Ted Lindsay came in third, followed by Bernie "Boom-Boom" Geoffrion, Bert Olmstead, Red Kelly, and Dutch Reibel. Ted, Red, and I were also First Team All-Stars, while Sawchuk made the Second Team. Doug Harvey, Ken Mosdell, and the Rocket made the All-Star Team for the Canadiens. With that much firepower clustered between our teams, it wasn't a surprise when we ended up squaring off for the Stanley Cup. Both semifinals went quickly. Montreal swept Boston while we put away Toronto in five games.

As I have already said, the Red Wings didn't like the Canadiens and they didn't like us. By 1954, Montreal's playoff roster contained the core of their team for years to come. The Rocket, Geoffrion, Olmstead, Mosdell, Harvey, Jean Béliveau, and Jacques Plante were all contributing on a nightly basis. We respected their talent, but that's where any semblance of fondness ended. The feelings went both ways. If you were walking toward the Rocket, he'd cross the street just to avoid talking to the enemy. During a playoff series or when the league scheduled a home-and-home, the teams would sometimes find themselves on the same train. Those trips could get tense. I don't think any fights ever broke out, but it came close. The conductor tried to keep the peace by scheduling us in the club car at different times, to keep as much distance between us as possible. Whoever coined the phrase "familiarity breeds contempt" could have been talking about the NHL during the six-team era. Between the regular season and the playoffs, we faced each other so often that hostility really had time to take root. And, boy, did it ever. Up and down both rosters, players had scores to settle with guys on the other bench. I wouldn't say we hated the Canadiens (except for Ted Lindsay; he probably did), but we sure harbored a healthy dislike for them.

The opening game of the series went according to plan. Pulling a rabbit out of his bag of coaching tricks, Tommy decided to move Delvecchio back to the Production Line. Playing with Alex felt like slipping on an old shoe. The team didn't miss a beat and we took the first game 3–1. Montreal won the second game, and then we came back to take the next two at the Forum. Up 3–1 in the series, we had the Habs on the ropes. Trying to find a spark, Dick Irvin benched Jacques Plante for Gerry McNeil. He hadn't seen much action in a while, but he was so sharp you couldn't tell. He turned out to be the edge the Habs needed and they took the next two, to even the series at three games apiece.

Game seven was exactly how you dream it will be when you're a little kid. The Olympia was packed. Nerves were running high in the dressing room and guys were keyed up to play. The game didn't disappoint once the puck dropped. Throughout the series, Tommy had assigned little Tony Leswick to check the Rocket. I can only imagine how much Maurice must have hated it. Tony might have been small, but he was strong on his skates and as tough as nails. He was also a player, made from the same mold as an Esa Tikkanen, who lived to get under your skin. I'd experienced the treatment firsthand when Tony was a Ranger. Not only did he become the Rocket's shadow that night, but he also chirped at him for the whole game. He called him Richard, using the English pronunciation. Richard this and Richard that, and "Hey, Richard, you're not going to score tonight." Some guys have a special switch in their heads that lets them be like that. They aren't fun to play against, but they're good to have on your side. I think it's the reason why Mr. Adams traded for Tony in the first place. If you can't beat 'em, join 'em.

At the end of regulation time, we were tied at 1–1. Overtime was only fitting for such a hard-fought series. Given all of the offensive talent on both benches, the Cup-winning goal came from an unlikely source. Doug Harvey had just cleared the puck when Leswick hopped over the boards on a line change in the second overtime. When he hit the ice, the puck was right there—and so was the Rocket, who had Tony lined up for a big hit. Tony, who didn't exactly have a cannon for a shot, flipped one toward the net as he tried to duck the Rocket's check. The puck was floating through the air so slowly that Harvey later said he could read the label on it as it came toward him. Doug was a great athlete. He'd played Double A baseball and probably could have made the big league if it wasn't for hockey. He moved to knock the puck out of the air and drop it on his stick, but it must have been knuckling a bit and he misjudged it. Instead of fielding it cleanly, he deflected it off the side of his glove. In net, Gerry McNeil was in position to make a routine save, but Harvey changed the puck's angle just enough that it floated past McNeil for the game-winner. The whole building was stunned: the crowd, both teams, Tony, Doug, and especially Gerry. It was our third Stanley Cup in five years and the second time we'd beat the Canadiens in the finals. And, of all people, we had little Tony Leswick to thank for it. Who would have thought?

When Jack Adams ended my baseball career a few years earlier, I didn't think there'd ever come a time when I didn't miss it during the summer. Wouldn't you know it, having a family changed all that. Instead of going back to Saskatoon that summer, Colleen and I were kept occupied by our new baby boy in Detroit. As busy as we were with Marty, however, I still managed to find some time to sneak away for a bit of an off-season baseball fix. Back then, a lot of the professional athletes in Detroit knew each other. I became so friendly with some of the Tigers that they'd invite me out for batting practice. One time, I remember that Don Lund was hanging some fat pitches out over the plate during BP, and I turned some heads by sending a few into the upper deck of old Briggs Stadium. The left-field stands where those balls landed were known as Greenberg Gardens, named after the legendary Hammerin' Hank Greenberg, who deposited his share of balls up there. I like to think that a few of the pitches I hit were for all of the good baseball players in Saskatchewan who never got a chance to take a cut in a big league park. That same day, I also met Al Kaline for the first time. The guys called me over and told me to watch the kid in right field. After catching a fungo, this whip of a kid would fire a picture-perfect one-hopper back to the catcher every time. He ran like an antelope and had such a beautiful throwing motion that it was easy to see he was something special. Al's talent was so great that I remember feeling a bit nervous when we were introduced, even though I was older and an established veteran in my own sport. We ended up becoming pretty good friends. Al, it should be mentioned, went on to be inducted into the Baseball Hall of Fame.

A few years later, I actually went into business with Al, but unfortunately it was a short-lived partnership. Detroit's auto industry was booming and Lindsay, Pavelich, and I formed a company with a local businessman to sell parts. My growing family could use every extra dollar we could get, and I thought the idea had good potential. Ted and Marty eventually broadened their interests into manufacturing, which is when I brought Al into the arrangement. Our outside business interests didn't sit well with Jack Adams, however. Articles that suggested we were paying more attention to our bank accounts than to hockey started popping up in the local paper. The accusation was ridiculous. Not only were we hockey players first and foremost but also we weren't pulling any money out of the business. That Mr. Adams would plant such stories and also have the nerve to take us to task through the press set Colleen's teeth on edge. Without telling me what they were up to, she and Pat Lindsay decided that since they were so rich, they might as well dress the part. They raided their Monopoly sets for fake bills, borrowed some mink stoles, and turned up at the next home game dressed as high rollers. The local photographers caught them lighting cigarettes with their Monopoly money and ran the photos the next day with a cutline that said, "Wives Pan Adams'

Comments." I don't think Mr. Adams ever forgave Colleen for that stunt. He was furious. The hassle that resulted from ticking off management eventually became too much and I decided to sell my stake in the business. I knew it wasn't the best move financially, but it did improve my life at the arena, which was worth something.

I would have liked to buy Colleen a fur coat of her own, but money was still a bit too tight. We were hardly living hand-to-mouth, but it wasn't like we had a lot of extra cash to splash around either. Around 1950 or '51, I had managed to save enough to buy my parents a new house in Saskatoon. My folks never had much, so to be able to do that for them was one of the great joys of making it to the NHL. I was at that house a few years later for a barbecue when my dad looked at me and asked, "What in the hell is the world coming to? We used to cook indoors and go to the bathroom outdoors." My dad could be really funny. Unfortunately, along with his sense of humor he also had a stubborn side. When I asked him to put the house in my name so I could pay the taxes and then write them off as a deduction, Dad's pride wouldn't let him do it. The old mule. When I gave my folks money, I always went through Mum and told her to keep it under her hat. I wish I could have sent them even more than I did in those years, but after Mark arrived in May 1955 we didn't have much to spare. Raising two kids meant we really had to keep track of our dollars and cents. Colleen made a household budget and we stuck to it like gospel.

A luxury that Colleen would have loved was a second car, but our financial situation kept us a one-vehicle family for many years. Another car would have made her life a lot easier. Being married to an NHL player had its perks, but I'm sure it was also a challenge.

Not only were we on the road during the season, but we'd disappear for training camp and again in the spring during playoffs. In the fall of 1955, Colleen found herself with a toddler, a new baby, no car, and a husband away at training camp in Sault Ste. Marie, Ontario. Looking back at her letters from that time makes it easy to appreciate how much of the family business she handled so I could concentrate on hockey.

*September 13, 1955*

*Hi Honey—*

*Phoned the AAA and Kotcher a while ago and here's the news. The AAA said to be sure to get a bill for the temporary repairs on the car from the Sault dealer so they can reimburse us for the money or pay it if you haven't already. Mr. Kotcher said he would give us these deals:*

| | |
|---|---|
| *On a '55 Convertible* | *$3,900 minus $1000 for our car* |
| | *$2,900 full price* |
| *On a '55 88 Deluxe* | *$3,650 minus $850 for our car* |
| | *$2,800 full price* |
| *On a '55 Ninety-eight* | *$4,100 minus $1200 for our car* |
| | *$2,900 full price* |

*What do those prices sound like? That's quite a bit of money! Should we wait for a '56 or not? I think so! This means, of course, we don't pay off the house, but it should only take us to next winter. But that should be all right. Miss you lots, Honey, and time seems to drag when you're gone.*

*The kids are good so far and I have no kick coming. Hope you're not too sore from skating. Call me at the end of the week when you decide what you'd like to do. A '98 hardtop would be real nice. What do you think?*

*Bye for now. Hugs and kisses from your three babies.*

*I love you, Colleen*

*P.S. Mark is 19 pounds.*

<br>

*September 15, 1955*

*Hello honey—*

*Thought I'd drop you a note to remind you that you have three folks back here in Detroit who are very lonesome for you. One is asleep, the other on my lap bugging me and the last one is writing this letter.*

*Poor Marty, I feel so sorry for him in the morning. He goes in our room and says, "Where da? Where da?" while he looks all over the bed. He really misses you.*

*. . . I scrubbed half the basement and plan to enamel it when it dries. Then I'll do the other half some other day. It's too much time in one day.*

*Well, sweetie, that's the news for now. There's not too much to say. Don't get around much any more. Pat [Lindsay] said she might get me a car for next week. Maybe. Write if you get a chance. Haven't heard from you yet. Why not? Bye bye.*

*Love, Colleen and the boys*

*September 21, 1955*

*Hello darling—*

*It has cooled off a bit today and made it a lot easier to sleep so Marty had a real long nap this afternoon. He's been so good since you've been gone.*

*I called Aunt Elsie to see how the baby is and she said fine. They're going to bring him back Friday evening. Marty looks in his bed and says, "Where Tee-Tee?"*

*. . . Lilly gal called yesterday and invited Jake [Pavelich] and me over for dinner (spaghetti) on Thursday. It'll be nice to get out for a change. Stevie [Carr] said she'd watch Marty so it shouldn't cost me any money. I may have to take a cab, though, unless Jake offers me a ride.*

*. . . I called Pat about the car but her mother thinks her granddad wants to use it now. Sure glad I didn't plan on it.*

*The Munroes have been very nice. They've offered to take me to the store any time I wanted anything. I've gone up twice with Marty in the wagon alone because I didn't need very much.*

*. . . I sent in our house payment for this month and also an extra $1,000. That should cut us down to $4,800 so we're getting it down little by little. We have a little more than $4,900 in our account plus what's in our checking so we're pretty well set for the car and insurance policies for the year.*

*. . . How's your cold now honey? That's what you get for kissing those strange girls.*

*This time you pick out the car and the <u>color</u> so I don't get any complaints. Ha Ha. Just so it isn't green.*

*That's about all for now, honey, because someone's starting to bug me to play with them. I'll run out to mail this now. I sure miss you—hurry home, but be careful on the road. Bye for now.*

*I love you, Colleen*

*September 23, 1955*

*Hello darling—*

*Looks as though you fellows might be ushering between periods this season since the Olympia maintenance crew has voted to strike when their contract is up October 1st. They want 50 cents per hour more per shift. Wonder if they'll get it.*

*. . . Sure sad because I missed your call tonight . . . Stevie [Carr] said I missed you by about 10 minutes. Darn it anyway. I love talking to you so much.*

*Received your two letters today and it's so refreshing to know you miss and love me (and the boys) but mostly me. It's sure tough to be alone when you're in love. I should have a long discussion with J.A. [Jack Adams] some day about the importance of wives at Training Camp. That's a good idea you and Marty have of having us meet you up north. Pretty sneaky, eh what?*

*. . . Carol [Carlin] called and wants me to go to dinner tomorrow evening with her and Pat. We called Jake too but*

*you can tell Marty he's got a real conservative wife 'cause she said the budget won't allow her to go. Besides she's tired of driving all over because everyone is on the west side and she's so far away. I think I'll go though, since I haven't spent any money since you left and don't want to break any records.*

*Am kind of anxious to meet some of the new wives this year. If the fellows are all nice, I'm sure the gals will be, too. It'll be kind of nice to see some new faces.*

*Weeded out the garden today and have two huge brush piles to burn when you get home to help me. I don't want to light it when I'm here alone. Also transplanted one of Stevie's rose bushes on the fence on to our fence by the garage. Hope it takes because it's such a pretty one. That Stevie is one of the best! Got down and weeded your patio, too. There were quite a few little weeds sneaking in there to give us some trouble next spring so I gave them the blade. That back corner will be a good place for swings next year. We can get a small load of sand for it so we won't need a sandbox, either. By the way, I watered your grass that's coming up where you tore up the old sandbox.*

*So you guys are going up to Edmonton now! Fine thing! You save those goals for season games, honey the —— with those exhibition deals. Those aren't money-makers anyway.*

*. . . Before I close, honey, I want you to know that although I act kind of goofy sometimes, this gal is still as much or more in love with you as the first night we went out together—and that's really a lot. Hurry home, dear.*

*My love, Colleen*

(Colleen sent this during the first series of the Stanley Cup playoffs.)
[To Gordie Howe, c/o Red Wing Hockey Club, Hamilton, Ontario]

*March 25, 1956*

*Dear honey, baby sugar doll—*

*I haven't written you a letter in so long that I thought you might enjoy hearing from your lonely little wifey.*

*After you left on the bus, Teresa, Bev, Marlene, Irene, Bibs and I went to Harrison's for a sandwich. Just living it up all the time! Then we all went home to our lonely individual abodes to think of our sweet husbands and to wish they were with us instead of being so far away.*

*. . . It was a riot this morning—you should have seen it. I got up with the little angels (?) and got them breakfast. Then your sleepy wife tried to grab a little catnap. I slept about 15 minutes and during that time, Marty opened all the jello and pudding packages and poured them all over Mark, who was sitting there eating all he could cram into his mouth. It took me over an hour to undo what took them a matter of minutes. Then they both went into the tub for a complete shampoo and bath. Wish we would have had some flashbulbs here so I could have taken a shot of the picture that stood before me when I poked my head into the kitchen. The three of us just looked at each other and laughed. (My laughter was a bit on the hysterical side.) All the joys of motherhood!*

*I don't know how the weather is in Toronto, but right this minute Hal is shoveling eight inches of snow off your sidewalk. What a snow we've had today! I went out twice to knock some of the weight off the shrubs. There was so much snow on the branches, they were breaking and bending right to the ground. I'm going to the grocery store tomorrow on dogsled.*

*Well, dear, things here are pretty horrible without you. I'm really looking forward to going on our vacation together and as far as I'm concerned, it will be more than a second honeymoon, and much nicer than our first. No arguments! Maybe I can make it up to you for all the little bitching I do sometimes. Also maybe we can make up for some lost time on our love life (you'd go for that, eh?).*

*Anyway, I'll be very happy to have you home, dear, because I love you more than you'll ever know.*

*All my love, Colleen*

*P.S. What do you want for your birthday?*

In that era, NHL clubs didn't give much consideration to a player's home life. For Jack Adams, especially, wives and winning just didn't mix. During the playoffs, he was so fixated on eliminating any distractions that our wives became temporary widows. For home playoff games, the club would pack us off to Toledo, which is about an hour's drive from Detroit. We'd stay cloistered there until shortly before game time, when we'd climb on a bus and head straight to the Olympia. Afterward we'd have a few minutes to sign autographs and, if we were lucky, say a quick hello to our wives before being hurried back on board the waiting bus. Colleen despised the arrangement. Why, she wondered, did we have to live like monks during the playoffs when we won games all year long while staying at home? It was a fair point. A good playoff run could stretch on for six weeks, which meant I'd practically have to reintroduce myself to our kids when I got home.

One year, when we opened the playoffs against Toronto, Colleen crafted a plan to deke out Mr. Adams. The club was keeping us stashed in a motel in Hamilton, which happened to be near some friends of ours, Ed and Agnes Taube. They invited Colleen and Pat Lindsay to visit. With some help from the Taubes, the wives booked themselves into a motel not far from ours. After the game, Ted and I managed to sneak away and rendezvous with our sweethearts. If Mr. Adams had caught us, we would have been in hot water, but it was worth the risk. Colleen got a real kick out of the whole illicit undertaking. She felt like we were a couple of teenagers running around behind our parents' backs. When we all left the next morning, I'm pretty sure the desk clerk recognized the pair of Red Wings skulking through the lobby. He probably assumed there was some hanky-panky going on. I think it would have disappointed him to learn that everything was so aboveboard. As we walked out, I leaned over to Colleen and whispered, "If you ever get an anonymous letter about my sleeping with some girl in a Hamilton hotel, you'll know it was you."

In the off-season before the start of the 1954–55 season, the team saw the beginning of changes that would affect us for years to come. In those days, the NHL, still largely unregulated, had arrangements that wouldn't fly today. Among them, the owners had a gentlemen's agreement to help bolster the lineups of the league's bottom feeders. It had cost us Sid Abel two years earlier and this time around we lost our coach, who became Chicago's new general manager. To make matters worse, not only did we lose Tommy

Ivan, but Metro Prystai was sent out the door along with him. To take over behind the bench, Mr. Adams called up Jimmy Skinner, who'd played under Tommy in Omaha before moving into Detroit's farm system as a coach, making stops in Windsor and Hamilton. I never thought Jimmy's understanding of the game was close to what Tommy brought to the table. It wasn't just Xs and Os, either. Tommy had also worked hard to insulate his players from the mood swings of their general manager. We lost that buffer once he left. From the start, we could tell that Jimmy Skinner was no Tommy Ivan. If a choice needed to be made between his players and his general manager, he was definitely going to be his boss's man in the dressing room.

The 1954–55 season is probably remembered better for what happened off the ice than on it. Hockey fans know all about the Richard Riot that broke out in Montreal, but they may not recall all of the events that led up to it. The roots of that crazy night can be traced back earlier in the season, to a game that had nothing to do with the Canadiens. We were playing in Maple Leaf Gardens when somehow I became mixed up with a fan who decided to lunge over the boards and take a swing at me. Ted, being Ted, wasn't about to let anybody—fan or otherwise—touch his linemate, so he skated over and cracked the guy with his stick. The league didn't like seeing a player hit a paying customer and suspended Ted for ten days, which cost him four games. As much as we didn't like the decision, the team moved past it in the best way we knew how and just kept piling up wins. By mid-March we found ourselves in a tight battle with Montreal for top spot in the standings. Finishing first would give us home-ice advantage in the playoffs, which is something we desperately wanted, given how well Montreal played at the Forum and how good we were at the Olympia.

With only a few games left in the regular season, the Canadiens made a fateful trip to Boston. During a game against the Bruins, the Rocket got into it with Hal Laycoe. After exchanging some pleasantries, Laycoe split open the Rocket's head with his stick. By all accounts, Maurice went a little nuts after that. He started chopping at Laycoe with his stick and Hal fought back with his own. A linesman managed to grab hold of the Rocket, but when he did, Laycoe took that as an opportunity to land a few free shots. Doug Harvey pulled the linesman off his teammate and that's when things really went downhill. Richard turned around and slugged the linesman, which, of course, is a serious no-no. Big star or not, the league threw the book at the Rocket. Detroit's management was especially adamant that the punishment fit the crime. Since Ted Lindsay had received a ten-day suspension for hitting a fan, Mr. Adams argued that the sanctions against Montreal's right winger needed to be even more punitive. It was hardly Richard's first offense. Earlier in the season, he'd cuffed a linesman, but come away with only a slap on the wrist. League president Clarence Campbell decided to send a message and suspended the Rocket for the final three games of the regular season and all of the playoffs. Around the league, players were stunned. Meanwhile, fans in Montreal weren't just shocked, they were angry.

The suspension came down on St. Patrick's Day, March 17, 1955. That same night, we were in Montreal to play the Habs. We were tied in the standings and both teams had been looking forward to this showdown for weeks. None of us could have guessed that the Rocket would be wearing street clothes. During warm-ups, the fans at the Forum seemed restless. Their agitation wasn't helped when we jumped out to a quick 4–1 lead. During the first period intermission, a fan approached league president Clarence Campbell with his hand outstretched as if to say hello. When Campbell went to shake it, the guy slapped him across the face. Someone punched the slapper and that's when all hell broke loose. A canister of tear gas was set off, which cleared the stands. Thousands of angry fans poured out of the Forum and into the streets, and the elegant city of Montreal had itself a proper riot—broken windows, overturned cars, gunfire, the whole nine yards. Of course, I heard about all of this secondhand. When the tear gas went off we were in our dressing room, busily stuffing wet towels under the door to keep out the smoke. A note was passed into the room telling us that the game was being forfeited and we'd get the win. We didn't ask any questions; we just dressed and got the hell out of town as quickly as possible. After all of that, the rest of the season felt like a formality. Our final game of the year was against the Canadiens at the Olympia. Back on home ice, we pounded them 6–0, which put us 2 points ahead of them in the standings. With that, we not only locked up our seventh straight league championship but also secured home-ice advantage throughout the playoffs.

In the semifinal round we swept Toronto in four games and Montreal took care of Boston in five. For the second year in a row we were facing off against the Canadiens for the Stanley Cup, and once again it was a series that would go seven games. This time around, however, they wouldn't have the Rocket. I like to think the result would have been the same whether he'd played or not. I'm equally sure that Montreal die-hards would tell me I'm wrong. If I had my way, we'd be able to find out, but in reality it's just one of those things in sports that we won't ever be able to know. At home at the Olympia for game seven, in front of a packed house of screaming fans, we ended up beating our rivals by a score of 3–1. The home-ice advantage we'd worked to secure all year long turned out to be crucial. Every game in that series was won by the home team. The victory marked our second consecutive Stanley Cup and our fourth in the last six years. We couldn't have been riding any higher, and we were already starting to think about our chances for three in a row. As it turned out, that idea turned out to be far too premature. Whoever said that you should treasure the moment, because no one knows what tomorrow will bring, knew a lot about life. I didn't know it at the time, but the 1955 Stanley Cup would be my last. Trader Jack was about to make some changes that put the organization into a hole so deep we couldn't find our way out of it.

*Eight*

# LIFE IN THE NHL

The host of a TV show once asked me if I was scared of anything. I thought for a second and then told him that lightning really put the fear of God in me. It was just an expression, but for some reason it brought out the altar boy in him and he interrupted to explain that I had it wrong because the Good Lord doesn't put fear into anybody. It felt to me like he was splitting hairs, so I said, "Wait a minute, he controls that lightning, and that scares the hell out of me." I felt the same way about the amount of control Jack Adams had over the Red Wings. He used to say, "I may not be right all the time, but I do sign the checks and that makes me right." It was tough luck for his players that, all too often, the checkbook was mightier than the hockey stick. If Mr. Adams thought you were a bad influence on the club, he'd ship you out the door, either down to the minors or to another team entirely. It didn't matter how good of a player you were or whether his paranoia had any basis in reality.

Mr. Adams was a divisive figure, to say the least. Even on the day of his funeral, when people are inclined to be charitable about the guest of honor, I remember swapping stories on the drive over to the cemetery about how he could be a mean old bugger. It went on like that for a while until someone piped up and began talking about the values Mr. Adams had instilled in his teams and how Jack's words had helped him in his post-hockey career. As true as that might have been, another former Red Wing in the car wasn't having any of it. He interrupted to offer a less generous assessment: "He was a miserable SOB and today he's a dead miserable SOB." That's what you got with Mr. Adams.

Over the years, Mr. Adams and I spent our fair share of time together. Away from the arena he had a different side than the one he showed to most of his players. At the end of each season, we used to drive up to northern Michigan on a publicity tour for Stroh Brewery. For a couple of weeks each year, Mr. Adams, myself, and Fred Huber, the club's head of public relations, would tour around the state showing a highlight reel of our season. Sometimes we'd do five showings in a day. At $25 a pop, the money added up in a hurry. At that time, any chance I had to supplement my family's income in the off-season felt like a real gift.

The teams kept a tight rein on what you could do to make money after the six-month hockey season ended. Your options for outside work were really hamstrung by the standard player's contract of the time. Making a few extra dollars by playing another sport, for instance, was against the rules, as I found out with baseball. Some of the luckier guys had family businesses they could return to, while others were relegated to picking up seasonal manual labor jobs where they could. For me, touring around with Mr. Adams and Fred and getting paid for my mileage by the brewery was a sweet deal. To put the money in perspective, consider how much we pulled down for winning a Stanley Cup. A first-round playoff win meant an extra $20,000 for the team. After the coaches, trainers, and scouts took their cut, it worked out to around $700 per player. If you went on to win the Cup, players would theoretically get another $2000 (the losing team got $1000 a man), but that was before agreeing to the split. All told, a successful playoff run would put around $2000 in your pocket before taxes. In a good year, playoff money could account for a significant chunk of your annual income, given that the average salary was around $6000 or $7000 at the time. In comparison, I could rack up nearly $1250 for a couple of weeks' work on the Stroh tour. And all I had to do was show movies; I didn't have to get hit. In light of today's salaries it may seem hard to fathom, but that was the state of the league at the time. The owners, with their business savvy, knew how to hang on to a dollar. Most players, in contrast, were happy just to get paid to play hockey, which doesn't exactly put you in a position of strength at contract time.

On the road in the spring, Mr. Adams could be a decent enough guy, but his bullying nature would reemerge once he returned to his desk at the Olympia. He chose to rule his team with an iron fist, which was just fine with the team's owner. Since taking over the club in the 1930s, James Norris, who was known as Pops, had solidified himself as the league's most influential owner. His authority was backed by his great wealth, as well as by the direct or indirect stakes he held in three of the league's six clubs: the Wings, the Rangers, and the Black Hawks. Such a conflict of interest wouldn't pass muster these days, but at the time the league's dealings often happened in the shadows. When it came to matters of hockey, Norris trusted Mr. Adams, which gave Jack free rein with the club. In return for the owner's faith and deep pockets, Mr. Adams managed to put a winning team on the ice more often than not.

When Pops died in late 1952, few people took it harder than Mr. Adams, who saw him as something of a father figure. They'd talked on the phone after every game, with Mr. Adams either reporting the good news of a victory or breaking the bad news if we'd lost. With Norris gone, control of the Red Wings passed to his daughter, Marguerite. Her role with the team has been relegated to a footnote in sports history, but I think she was the first woman to ever run a professional team. I don't know how Mr. Adams felt about his new team president, but I'm sure he wasn't thrilled about a woman in her twenties handing down his marching orders. Regardless, since her brothers Jimmy and Bruce owned shares in the Black Hawks, the family needed to put someone in the role and the job fell to her. In the time I spent around Marguerite, I found her to be both smart and capable. Others I talked to felt the same way. She was good for the club, but unfortunately she didn't stick around for as long as anyone would have liked. A few years into the job, she was ousted by her older brother, Bruce. She became the club's executive vice president, but her involvement didn't last much longer. In retrospect, it's easy to see how bad the family infighting was for the team. Marguerite was a much more thoughtful owner than her brother, who could be something of a bully.

I don't think it's a coincidence that Marguerite's time in charge coincided with some of the greatest years in franchise history. As president, she had enough juice to check Trader Jack's instincts to upset the apple cart. It's hard to say how many Stanley Cups we might have won if she had stuck around longer. In my mind, the ingredients were in place to form one of the greatest dynasties in hockey history. Sadly, we weren't left alone for long enough to find out what might have been. Bruce's hockey acumen was no match for his sister's, which was good for Mr. Adams but bad for the rest of us. Despite winning seven consecutive league championships and two straight Stanley Cups, Trader Jack decided to spend the 1955 off-season dismantling the team.

To this day, his reasons for blowing up our championship squad defy explanation. First, he sent Tony Leswick, Johnny Wilson, Glen Skov, and Benny Woit to the Black Hawks for Bucky Hollingworth, Dave Creighton, Jerry Toppazzini, and John McCormack. The deal was a real Norris brothers special. Bruce gift-wrapped four top-tier players and sent them to his brother Jimmy's team in Chicago. What's worse, Mr. Adams wasn't done. A week later he dealt Terry Sawchuk, Vic Stasiuk, Marcel Bonin, and Lorne Davis to the Bruins for Warren Godfrey, Ed Sandford, Réal Chevrefils, and a couple of rookies. In the newspapers, Mr. Adams said he needed to make room on the roster for young players like Johnny Bucyk and Norm Ullman. He also had Glenn Hall parked in Edmonton waiting to take over in net. Hall was a terrific goaltender, no question, but trading Sawchuk, who was coming off another Vezina Trophy, was hard to swallow. Most general managers spent their entire career waiting for a goalie like Sawchuk, who they could build a team around, to come along. Not Mr. Adams. When Terry was on his game, it's hard to think of anyone better. He also always seemed to save his best for when the stakes were the highest. An NHL team can't ask for much more than having a goalie who heats up every spring.

By the time the smoke cleared, Trader Jack had dealt away half of our team. Only nine of us remained from a squad that had raised the Stanley Cup a few short months earlier. Looking back, I'd say the ball started rolling downhill when we lost Sid Abel and Tommy Ivan. It picked up speed when Bruce Norris pushed out Marguerite, which paved the way for Trader Jack's maniacal 1955 off-season. Those trades turned out to be the final straw. I have a hard time thinking about what might have been. I think a lot of my old teammates feel the same way. For the rest of the league, the opposite is probably true. The upheaval in our roster was good news for everyone else. No one took more advantage of the new power vacuum on top of the league than the Canadiens. The dismantling of the Red Wings juggernaut cleared the way for Montreal, who went on to win five Cups in a row. Without the trades, would we have beaten them in any of those years? No one can say for sure, but our track record until that point suggests we would have at least given them a run for their money. We were still competitive, but it's easy now to see how those trades sapped us of the firepower we needed to win another championship.

Some sports fans are turned off by the multimillion-dollar contracts signed by today's athletes. The sharp escalation in salaries certainly has put many players out of touch with the average Joe, but—be that as it may—I'm here to tell you that the good old days weren't as good as you might think. Fans may see the rise of so-called super agents and management companies as being bad for the game, but before they showed up, players didn't have anyone looking out for their best interests. The playing field was tilted, and that's exactly the way the league liked it. Most of us had quit high school to play junior hockey, which turned us into good players but didn't do much for us at the negotiating table. And the owners didn't miss a trick when it came to maintaining the status quo. Players were kept in the dark about the business side of the game, which allowed clubs to peddle whatever story they wanted about their financial situation. Most of them claimed they were just scraping by and that we were all lucky to have jobs. Of course, they never showed us any proof, and even if they had cracked open the books, the numbers wouldn't have made much sense to most of us. It wasn't until years later that we learned how much money the league was really making, but by then it was too late to do much about it.

When it came time to negotiate a new contract, players didn't have much of a frame of reference. Contractually, we were obliged to stay quiet about our salaries, even when talking to our teammates. This gave the owners a big leg up and they knew it. They turned it into such an ingrained part of the league's culture that players just accepted the idea that discussing salaries was off-limits. I probably have less to complain about than most. Since I was one of the better players in the game, Mr. Adams had a vested interest in keeping me happy. I wish I'd made it harder for him, but at my core, I was still just grateful to be playing hockey for a living. Talking about money is also uncomfortable for a lot of people, and I was no exception. I think Mr. Adams was aware of that little piece of social psychology and used it to his advantage. If I was happy to get out of his office as quickly as possible, he wasn't going to stop me.

The owners, unlike their players, understood the power of information. When I sat down at the table with Mr. Adams, he had all of it and I had none. When he assured me I'd be the best-paid player on the Red Wings and probably the highest-paid player in the NHL, I didn't have any reason not to believe him. He didn't know exactly what other teams paid their players, he claimed, but he promised he would always do his best to ensure that my salary reflected my stature in the league. It seemed fair to me. Multiyear contracts didn't exist at that point, so at the end of training camp every year I'd sit down in his office and we'd come up with a new one-year deal. Most seasons, he'd offer me $1000 more than my previous salary and I'd sign. He also included bonus incentives, which made sense to my way of thinking. I figured that if I had a good season, it meant the team would succeed as well. One year—I think it was 1952—I basically doubled my salary through bonuses. I took home the Hart Trophy and the scoring title, I was named to the All-Star Team, and we won the Stanley Cup. The total haul came to an additional $9000 or so.

To my dismay, I've since realized that I was far too trusting of management in those days. When Mr. Adams assured me I was the league's highest-paid player, I was inclined to believe him. If I was naive, then management certainly did its part to keep me that way. The clubs did everything they could to keep salaries in check. If they didn't like the cut of your jib, there was always another farm boy from the Prairies just waiting for the call to the big leagues. Even for the top guys in the game, it felt like you were never more than one loose comment or one unlucky injury away from being out of the league. In retrospect, I should have been more of a hard case, but if I'm being completely honest with myself, I know that being an agitator isn't in my nature. I guess I also bought into all of the talk of the Red Wings being a family. If I put in an honest day's work, I thought Mr. Adams could be trusted to pay an honest day's wage. That's what he promised, anyway. Other players, like Ted Lindsay, were much less willing to take his word at face value.

In professional sports today, collective bargaining agreements and players' unions are par for the course. The world was entirely different in the 1950s. It was a time of McCarthyism, the House Committee on Un-American Activities, and the Hollywood blacklist. Among the general public, the mere mention of the word "union" wasn't going to win you many friends. Although few players realized it, the owners were taking such great advantage of us that a union was exactly what we needed. Whether we were ready to join one was another matter. Ted Lindsay's first taste of league business came in 1955, when he and Doug Harvey were selected to represent the players on the board of the National Hockey League Pension Society. Regardless of how many times they asked, the league wouldn't furnish any information about the size of the pension fund or how its investments were performing. The league assured the players that its pension plan was the gold standard in professional sports, which we were counting on, since the $900 a year we paid into it represented a significant portion of our take-home pay. Getting stonewalled when he tried to verify those claims didn't sit well with Lindsay. He developed a suspicion about the owners that wouldn't go away.

In the 1956 off-season, Lindsay bumped into Cleveland Indians pitcher Bob Feller, who was also the president of the Major League Baseball Players Association. The chance encounter tipped off Lindsay to the contract that baseball players had just received from their owners. Wanting to learn more, Lindsay met with the lawyers who had negotiated that deal. Over the course of several meetings, they concocted a plan. At the All-Star Game that next season, Lindsay approached Harvey and they came up with the seeds of what would become the NHL's first players' association. A select group of veteran players quietly signed up nearly every player in the league. When they were finally ready, Lindsay held a press conference to tell the world—and the owners—about the new association. It went poorly right off the bat. The owners were furious. In Detroit, Jack Adams was apoplectic. At a hastily convened team meeting he spat words like "loyalty," "family," and "betrayal" at us. He wanted to bully us into feeling guilty about turning our backs on the league's benevolent ownership. In reality, the owners felt threatened by the new association. It wasn't until years later that we learned how intent they had been to break it up.

The league launched a coordinated campaign to feed misleading information to the press, the public, and even the players. Teams in each city cracked down on anyone who was perceived to be sympathetic to the cause. In our dressing room, that started with Lindsay. In the summer of 1957, he was shipped to the Black Hawks along with Glenn Hall. On paper, the deal didn't make any sense. Both players had been First Team All-Stars the year before and Ted had been the league's second-leading scorer with 85 points. Of course, on-ice performance wasn't the point. Over time, nearly everyone considered to be a ringleader in the new players' association was either traded or drummed out of the league. Not even Marty Pavelich, who wasn't particularly active in the players' association, was spared. Mr. Adams made Marty, who was Ted's good friend and business partner, into an example by demoting him to the minor leagues. Marty wasn't having any of it. With Ted in Chicago, no one would be around to look after their business interests if he left Detroit. He refused to accept the unjust transfer and instead, at only twenty-nine years old, went into a forced retirement. It was dirty pool by Mr. Adams, but he didn't care. The owners were playing hardball. Rumor had it that Marguerite tried to oppose the trades, but she was railroaded by her brother into standing pat. She gave up her executive duties shortly after and that was the last we saw of her around the Red Wings.

Around the league, other teams were doing their part to break up the players' solidarity. The players' association eventually fought back by filing an antitrust suit against the owners. Our locker room wasn't sure that was the best move. A lawsuit seemed like a precursor to a strike, and we believed that further negotiations were in order before we went that far. Before choosing to support the antitrust suit, we wanted to know more about its potential consequences. After a team vote, we decided not to strike. Without a mandate from one of the league's six teams, the players' association was put in a tough spot. The solidarity didn't last much longer and the association disbanded after the owners made a few face-saving concessions and some vague promises to treat us better in the future. Looking back, it's easy to say now that we should have shown more resolve when the owners tried to crack us. I also accept that the situation might have turned out differently if I had taken on a larger leadership role. To be honest, though, I know that my heart wasn't in organizing my teammates and fighting the owners. I just wanted to play hockey. Today, players are willing to stand up for what's right, and I admire that. The waters were much murkier in the 1950s. Strikes were considered to be almost a communist activity. That was a tough perception to overcome. As someone who played in that era, I can also say that we weren't nearly as well equipped to understand the bigger picture. It makes me happy to see how much things have changed.

As a footnote to all of this, I should probably add a word about my relationship with Ted Lindsay. Before he was traded to Chicago, our friendship had been deteriorating for some time. In our early days with the Red Wings, we were as thick as thieves. Not only did we room together at Ma Shaw's, but he was also in my wedding party and I even lived in his house after he married Pat. I have some remorse about how things turned out, but I also know that nothing lasts forever. Not even friendships. The cracks in ours probably started when we went into business together. Ted said some things about me to our partners that were hard for me to get past. I'm sure I did some things he didn't like too much, either. After his trade to Chicago and the whole rigmarole with the players' association, mending fences became that much harder. Our relationship deteriorated further when I was in talks to return to the Red Wings shortly after he took over as the team's general manager in the 1970s. We're civil enough when we run into each other but, given the number of differences we've had over the years, our contact is limited to a handshake. That doesn't stop me from smiling when I think about the good times we shared, but they were long ago. In the years since, I've had plenty of time to consider the nature of friendship. These days, I think of Ted as someone I once played with on a line and not much more.

As time went on, the success that the Wings had long enjoyed became frustratingly elusive. The other teams in the league were too good for us to be able to overcome the string of lopsided trades and mismanagement. No matter how tough things got at the arena, though, I could always take solace in coming home to our growing family. I really didn't get to know my father, who worked all the time when I was a kid, until I was much older. I knew I wanted to have a different relationship with my children. I like to think I managed fairly well for the most part, even if it wasn't always as easy to pull off as I would have liked. If I had one quibble with playing professional hockey, it was the amount of traveling. I didn't mind being on the road, per se, but leaving Colleen and the kids so often was hard. I missed more track meets, hockey games, and recitals than I would have liked, but I always got the play-by-play as soon as I came home. By and large, though, I don't mind sounding boastful when I say that I think Colleen and I did a pretty fine job when it came to parenting.

Since our first two kids still had all their fingers and toes, we figured the family could survive another addition or two. In the spring of 1959, we introduced Marty and Mark to their new baby sister, Cathy. A year and a half later, we welcomed their little brother, Murray, to the family. Growing up, it was only natural that our kids found themselves around a lot of hockey. They would scamper around the Olympia like it was their second home. I remember toting Mark into the dressing room with me once after a game. We'd had a few losses in a row, which made Mr. Adams miserable. He came storming into the room, hollering and screaming and chucking pieces of orange at us. When he paused for breath, the room was so quiet you could hear a pin drop. With the impeccable timing that comes only with being five years old, Mark picked that moment to ask, "Hey, Dad, who's that big fat guy?" My teammates deserve a medal for holding back their laughter. Mr. Adams didn't say anything; he just tied up his rant and left the room. As soon as the door closed behind him, everyone nearly busted a gut. About a week later, Mr. Adams informed us that kids would no longer be allowed in the dressing room on game days. The team called it the Mark Howe rule.

Colleen and I gave our kids a lot of leeway in making their own choices. We didn't believe in punishment as much as in trying to instill discipline through mutual respect, and figured that guidelines were more effective than hard-and-fast rules. That was our philosophy, anyway. For instance, once they were older, we never had a curfew in place. If they were going to be home later than expected, we just asked that they call and let us know. We did the same for them.

I always hoped our kids would share my love of hockey, but Colleen and I agreed that we'd never push the sport (or anything else, for that matter) on them. They'd have our full support and encouragement regardless of what they chose to do. It would be lying to say I don't feel lucky about how things turned out. Our three boys took to hockey like fish to water. Showing up at the rink as Gordie Howe's sons wasn't always easy for each of them, but they handled it in stride. I would have loved to have seen Cathy with a stick in her hand, too, but women's hockey wasn't on the radar like it is now (and, by the way, women today can really play). She preferred running to skating, anyway. I loved seeing her beat the boys in a footrace when she was a kid and then watching her fly around the track as she got older. In high school she ran the anchor leg for the 220- and 440-yard relays (which are now the 200 and the 400). She also ran the 220 on her own and competed in shot put. That lasted only until she dropped a shot and broke all of the bones in her foot. She spent a long year watching the rest of that track season from the sidelines.

Right from the start, Mark, who could recite stats for all the players in the league, was always the biggest hockey nut. He was constantly running outside with a stick in his hand, either to bang pucks against the garage door or to talk a neighborhood kid into playing goalie for him. He really took after his old man that way. Marty always liked the game, but he didn't approach it with the same single-minded focus as Mark. He might have loved football just as much, but he was eventually forced to give it up. When he was in high school, Marty's football coach made him choose between playing in a big hockey game or attending football practice. He picked hockey and the coach dismissed him from the team. I respect commitment, but it seemed clear in that instance that high school football took itself too seriously. The coach should have lightened up. We always wondered what would have happened if Marty hadn't given it up. He was a heck of a player and I think he would have been good enough to play football in college.

Born just fifteen months apart, Marty and Mark were close as kids, often sharing a room. Like any pair of brothers, they could also fight like cats and dogs, but their arguments didn't last long and they were always there for each other when it mattered. One day, when Mark was still only in preschool, I remember him barreling into the house to tell me that a boy was picking on Marty. I was only half paying attention, so I told him that instead of letting some kid beat up his brother, he should clunk him on the head with a hockey stick. I went back to reading the paper, until I saw Mark flash out the door with a stick in his hand. Stupid me: I should have been listening instead of giving him a thoughtless answer. I hightailed it into the street and caught Mark just before he clobbered the kid with his stick. I learned a good parenting lesson that day. But it was comforting to see them stick up for each other when needed. I used to tell them that friends will come and go, but your family would always be there for you. The lesson seems to have stuck, I'm happy to say. Their loyalty also extended beyond their siblings. Mark was still little when he wrote this letter to me while I was on the road.

*Dear Daddy,*

*We had practis at 7 in the morning. Mrs. V. drove us to the skating club. Thursday we are going to bramton. If you win the Stanley Cup we will win in bramton. i am glad you beat up the man in Chicago. He could not beat you up if he tried. i hope you have a happy birthday.*

*Sincerely,*
*Mark Howe*

I was glad that I beat up the man in Chicago, too. He was a jerk and he'd deserved it. I also thought that Mark's decision to end his letter with "sincerely" was a nice touch for a nine-year-old.

Our youngest son, Murray, was a good hockey player in his own right, but he never reached quite the same level as his brothers. His mother and I never wanted to discourage him from playing hockey, but we were pretty sure his career path would be away from the ice. When he was little, he just wanted enough space to play with his toy soldiers in a spot where his brothers wouldn't knock them over. Later on, he was always looking for a place where he could sit quietly and read a book. In school, his report card was filled with As and he was a permanent fixture on the honor roll. Even as a rug rat, he was so crafty and smart we figured he might have a future in law. I remember teasing him one day about sucking his thumb. I told him if he didn't keep it out of his mouth, it would fall off. He was a sensitive kid and didn't like being teased by his dad. He was so upset that he went directly upstairs and asked Colleen for my address at the Olympia. She thought it was for a friend who wanted to write a fan letter, so she gave it to him. Little did she know the address was for Murray, and at that moment he wasn't much of a fan. When I picked up my mail at the arena a few days later, the handwriting on one of the envelopes looked suspiciously like my five-year-old's. The letter inside simply said:

*Dear Dad,*
*    I do not like you.*

*Love,*
*Murray*

By the time I confronted him about the letter, he'd forgotten all about it. He didn't even remember why he'd been mad. Thinking he was in trouble, he became pretty nervous. Credit to my son, though: He kept his composure. He took the letter from me and stared at it like he was cracking a code. His face finally brightened and then he handed it back. "Don't you get it, Dad?" he asked. "I don't like you—I *love* you!" After that bit of fancy footwork, we figured maybe politics was in his future. Turns out we were wrong. He went on to become Dr. Murray Howe, MD.

Before Murray was even a twinkle, let alone a radiologist, I was lucky enough to share a very special night with the members of my family I didn't get to see nearly often enough. I'd spent thirteen years in the NHL, but my parents hadn't had a chance to watch me play professional hockey. My dad worked so much when I was a kid, I'm not sure he ever even saw me play a game in Saskatoon. Parents didn't have time to cart their children around to games and practices. Kids took care of themselves without nearly as much involvement from parents as there is now. It would have been nice if my dad could have turned up to watch me, but it just wasn't in the cards. That changed for the better in March 1959, when the

Red Wings decided to hold a night of appreciation in my honor. I was flattered, to say the least. The on-ice presentation happened between periods, and as team officials called me to center ice. I remember thinking how much I would have liked my parents to be there. Even then, I still wasn't making enough money to bring them to Detroit easily, and they couldn't afford to come on their own. My mom hadn't been there since she'd come to take care of me in the hospital nearly ten years earlier. As for my dad, he wasn't too interested in venturing out of Saskatchewan. Whenever I brought it up, he'd just joke that it would be tough to get away because they didn't have anyone to feed the dog.

The club didn't spare any expenses for Gordie Howe Night, going so far as to line up about $10,000 worth of gifts, including clothes, a paid vacation, and toys for the kids. The capper was a new Oldsmobile. They'd wrapped the station wagon in cellophane and stuck a bow on it, and then driven it onto the ice. When I went to unwrap it, who do you think was sitting in the car? My parents. The team had flown them in secretly and put them up in a hotel. There I was at center ice, supposedly some big tough hockey player, and I was overwhelmed with emotion. I felt so proud that my parents could be there for that moment. I was still pretty choked up when they handed me the microphone to say a few words. Standing there with my mother and father, I was having trouble fighting back the tears. Even thinking about it now can bring a tear to my eye. I took the microphone and said the only thing that came to mind: "It's a long way from Saskatoon." Standing in front of thousands of fans at the Olympia, I felt a million miles away from the little guy who'd grown up sliding around the potato patch. At the same time, looking at my parents brought me right back home again. Taking stock of my life that night, I didn't have any complaints. At home, we had two beautiful, healthy kids and Colleen was about to give birth to our third. At the arena, things had gone almost as well. The team had won four Stanley Cups in my time and we had hopes for some more. By that time, I'd spent thirteen years in the NHL, which was already considered a long career. Although I already felt like the old man in the dressing room next to my younger teammates, I couldn't have dreamed how much more hockey I still had left to play.

*Nine*

# THE RECORD BOOK

W hen the NHL expanded to twelve teams in 1967, I remember thinking how much it changed the feel of the league. Doubling the number of teams gave a whole generation of players a chance to crack into the NHL on rosters that hadn't existed when fellas of my vintage were coming up. Playing in a league of thirty teams, as they do today, would be something else entirely. In the six-team era, you got to know everyone on the ice pretty quickly, for better and worse. A seventy-game schedule meant that teams faced each other fourteen times a year. Add to that a seven-game playoff series or two and you ended up playing a lot of hockey against the same faces. Not too many nights went by that you didn't have a history with at least a few guys on the other bench. The league was hungry back then. With only six teams, not only was it hard for a player to make it to the NHL but, once you broke in, you also had to fight like hell to stay there. Every season brought a new crop of young players looking to make their mark. They didn't want to go back down to the minors and the veterans weren't about to let anyone take food off their tables. No one gave an inch.

The circumstances are different today. I'm not saying players aren't tough, because they are. One look at their size tells you that much. Their understanding of diet and conditioning is also miles ahead of where we were. In my era, I was one of the bigger guys at six feet tall. Nowadays, I'd be average at best. It's easy to see why things have changed. Instead of just bird-dogging in small-town Canada, scouts now go around the world hunting for talent. Drawing from a global pool means that the size, speed, and skills of the players in the NHL just keep going up. The league is no longer composed of just the best Canadians and Americans, but also the top Russians, Swedes, Finns, Czechs, Germans, Slovenians, Slovakians, Latvians, and others. It makes for good hockey, but it's also a different game than the one we played. To be honest, I don't think it's as tough. That's not the same as saying that today's players aren't tough, just that the game itself has changed. When there were only six teams, every player in the league came prepared to claw over his best friend the second the puck dropped. With every NHL job being so precious, the play itself had an intensity that hasn't been seen since. Facing each other so often only ratcheted up the potential for animosity.

The most famous run-in I ever had was born out of those conditions. I was no stranger to fighting, particularly when I played in Omaha, but Detroit's management had long made it clear that if I had a choice, they'd rather keep me on the ice than see me in the penalty box. During a game in early 1959, New York's tough guy, Lou Fontinato, made sure I didn't have much of a choice. He consistently ranked among the NHL's leaders in penalty minutes and made it a point to tangle with anyone in the league who was considered tough. I guess you'd call him an enforcer. His coach figured that Louie irritated the hell out of me, so whenever I hit the ice he wanted him out there to try to take my head out of the game. At least one time, I remember, it worked just as they'd planned. I was so eager to get a piece of Louie that I forgot a valuable piece of Ted Lindsay's hockey wisdom: Always let the other guy drop his stick first. After banging on each other all night, Louie finally squared off with me and asked if I wanted to go. I was happy to oblige, so I threw my stick on the ice and dropped my gloves. Bad move. Louie still had his stick and he used it to split open my head for a few stitches. I knew that somewhere Ted was shaking his head at me. It's not a mistake I'd make again. Fool me once, as they say. As much as Louie and I went at each other, it took years before we actually settled things once and for all.

We were in New York playing the Rangers when Red Kelly got mixed up with Eddie Shack behind the net. I was watching them tussle when it dawned on me that I had better get a fix on Louie in case he was getting any ideas. When I turned around, sure enough his gloves and stick were at the blue line. He was about ten feet away and charging hard, obviously looking to do more than just say hello. I slipped my hands out of my gloves, just holding them with my fingertips, and waited for what was coming. He didn't know I had spotted him, so he figured he was swinging at a sitting duck. I moved just in time to miss the haymaker he threw at my head. I'm sure he was licking his chops at the thought of knocking me out with one big punch. Bill Gadsby, who was playing for the Rangers at the time, later told me that my career would have been over if

Louie had connected. To his surprise, I ducked the punch, dropped my gloves, and was ready to get it on.

Whenever I fought on the ice, I'd try to grab the other guy's sweater at the armpit of his power arm with my left hand. That would leave my right hand free to go to work and force him to throw with his weaker arm. It's the reason why fighting southpaws is so tricky. You instinctively go for the wrong arm. After ducking Louie's first punch, I tied up his right arm and started unloading on him with everything I had. I hit him as hard and as often as I could. The first few punches stunned him, but he managed to shake them off and land a few good lefts of his own. I didn't enjoy getting hit in the side of the head, so I switched hands and tied up the arm that was doing the damage. I was putting in some good work with my left hand, until one of my punches landed wrong and I dislocated a finger. It hurt like a son of a gun. When the officials separated us, I began to realize the kind of number I'd done on Louie. His face was covered with blood and his nose wasn't where it should have been. The whole thing was over in less than a minute, but the impression it left lasted much longer. Some of the reporters on hand described it as the worst beating they'd ever seen anyone take on the ice. I don't know if that's true, but the pictures afterward certainly didn't do Louie any favors. It didn't make me happy to see Louie in such bad shape, but I can't say I felt sorry for him. That might make me sound cold-hearted, but to my way of thinking he was just doing his job and I was doing mine. One of us was going to take the worst of it and it turned out to be him.

I'd say I probably get asked about that fight more than any of the goals I ever scored. I'd rather talk about the Stanley Cups and some of the great teammates I was lucky enough to play with, but I guess that scrap does have its place in the scheme of my career. No one was in much of a hurry to drop the gloves with me afterward, which was fine by me. I was grateful for anything that helped to keep me on the ice and out of the penalty box. Years later, I also learned a lesson from that night that didn't have anything to do with the fight itself. Back when we played together, Jack Stewart, a Wings defenseman, and Milt Schmidt of the Bruins used to have quite a hate on for each other. Every time we played the Bruins, they'd spend the whole night whacking at each other whenever they got a chance. I think neither one felt like he'd played a good game unless he'd drawn blood. It was pure meanness between those two. One night, I figured I'd give Jack a hand. I'd noticed that Milt would sometimes go up on one leg, like a dancer, to try to get by a defenseman on the outside. Jack wasn't too agile, so this often worked on him. For Milt, it was a gamble that left him off balance and vulnerable. I waited for my moment and when I saw Milt go up on one leg, I charged over and caught him perfectly. I figured that Jack would enjoy seeing his adversary take a good lick, but, boy, was I wrong. Between periods, he stormed into the dressing room, picked me right up off my seat, and said, "Young man, that's between that man and me. You stay the hell out of it." Then he dropped me back down. It took me years to understand what I'd done to make him so angry.

Later, after both men had retired, I was playing one night when I heard a commotion start to build in the crowd. I looked up and saw Jack and Milt in the stands. They'd spotted each other and walked through the rows of seats to shake hands. The whole audience rose in a standing ovation when they met. At that moment, I finally understood why Jack had been so stern with me in the dressing room that day. Whatever happened between those two was personal, and he didn't want anyone else muddying the waters. He didn't necessarily have to like Milt, but they respected each other. They were two professionals and playing hockey was their job. Win or lose, there's an honor that exists between combatants that he didn't want diminished.

After the game, I told Colleen how moved I was to see the sportsmanship embodied in that handshake. She pressed me and asked if I really felt that way. I told her I sure did. I should have recognized the look in her eyes at the time, but I didn't. You had to be careful with Colleen, because the wheels in her head were always turning. The chickens didn't come home to roost until some time later, when we were planning a trip to Vancouver for a charity banquet. It was a fund-raising event for disabled athletes and we were in charge of lining up some of the speakers. Colleen seized on the opportunity to remind me about Jack and Milt. If my feelings about their handshake were sincere, then she figured I should call up Louie and ask him to join us at the banquet in Vancouver. I didn't like the idea at first, but it started to make sense the more I thought about it. There wasn't really any bad blood between us; we had simply been two hockey players doing our jobs. I dialed his number and Louie and his wife joined us in Vancouver for a few days. After all those years of going at it on the ice, it's my pleasure to now call him a friend.

When I was at home with Colleen and the kids, it took a lot for me to lose my temper. I don't recall even raising my voice at our children that often, though I'm sure I did. Good as they may have been, our kids still weren't exactly angels all of the time. Even so, yelling and carrying on just wasn't in my nature. Colleen actually wished that I'd get more riled up sometimes. It bugged her, if she was fussed, that I'd remain calm. I rarely obliged her, though. I just loved her too much to sweat the small stuff. My even temperament threw her for a loop. She couldn't understand how I could be so easygoing at home, yet behave how I did on the ice. She thought I used the game as an outlet for my anger. I wasn't one to disagree for no reason, but her theory felt too much like dime-store psychology to me. Every player gets mad sometimes but, in general, anger wasn't a big part of my game.

What I learned early on was that you had to be a little crazy to survive in the NHL. And if you weren't crazy naturally, you needed to fake it a bit so your opponents thought you were. If you didn't, you became an easy target. I found that out the hard way. In my first NHL game, I had three teeth knocked out. From then on, if someone wanted to hit me in the mouth, I made sure they knew they'd have to come through some lumber to get there. I used to tell my boys that in order to get some respect on the ice, sometimes you needed to bend the rules. When I threw an elbow or got my stick up, it wasn't ever by chance and it was rarely out of malice. It was all about letting the other guy know not to take any liberties with me. The math was simple in my mind. Respect equals space. Being effective on the ice is a function of how much room you have to maneuver. The more room you get, the more games you can help your team win.

I was lucky that I didn't have to fake being crazy. It didn't matter who was across from me; I never thought twice about getting hurt. Even if a guy had some size on me, he never seemed that big once when we were on the ice. I didn't have any problem knocking down whoever was in my way. I figured that having the mindset that allowed me to play rough offered an advantage in hockey. The opposition is never too excited to tangle with someone who doesn't seem to care about getting hurt. A willingness to throw myself around the ice was one of the things that allowed me to stay in the league for so many years. Other players tended to give me a wide berth when I was on the ice, which is exactly what I wanted.

All that being said, it's not like it's anything goes when you're on the ice. Among the players I skated against, the ones I respected the most were those who understood what lines shouldn't be crossed. I played the game with a straightforward code. I didn't get into it with anyone who didn't have it coming. If someone played dirty, though, you'd better believe I took down his number. Payback might take a while, but when there was a score to settle I had a memory like an elephant. Whether it was the next game, five games down the road, or even the next season, I wouldn't forget. The way I saw it, if you didn't look out for yourself, no one would do it for you. If you let someone get away with something once, it was no one's fault but your own when it happened again.

Early in their careers, rookies often needed to be schooled quickly on what was acceptable and what wasn't. Many were so eager to make an impression that they'd fly around the rink with little regard for anyone. Sometimes they'd even look to earn their stripes by taking on an established player. As one of the guys near the top of that list, I knew that tolerating such behavior was just bad business. When Stan Mikita was coming up with Chicago, he had to learn that lesson the hard way. Stan turned into a great hockey player, but in his early days he took a little too much advice from Ted Lindsay, who by then was a veteran with the Black Hawks. Ted had Stan running around high-sticking guys. Regardless of what worked for Ted, that wasn't going to play for long. One night, Stan caught me in the mouth with his stick. He drew some blood, which never made me happy. Back on the bench, his teammates told him he shouldn't have done it. Apparently, he wasn't worried. He claimed there was no reason to be afraid of an old guy like me. Stan had a lot of moxie as a kid. Nevertheless, for the rest of the game he kept a close watch on me, just in case I had any bright ideas. He told me later, "I wasn't a dummy. I kept my eye out for you, and nothing happened." The next time we faced Chicago, I kept to myself. Another game went by with nothing from me but a smile. One more game passed and I still had no problem with Stan. It wasn't until the next time Chicago visited Detroit that I found my moment.

Stan was chasing me in our zone when I picked up the puck and hit Alex Delvecchio with a long pass that sent him in on the net by himself. As everyone else chased the play, Stan and I were left alone at the other end of the ice. He might have forgotten about the high stick, but I hadn't. I glided up next to him, pulled my hand out of my glove real fast, and popped him right between the eyes. He went down like a sack of potatoes. His teammates had to carry him to the bench. After the trainer gave him some smelling salts, the first person Stan saw when he came to was Denis DeJordy, Chicago's backup goaltender. Stan asked him what had happened. Denis just said, "Number 9." It was a real "welcome to the NHL" moment for Stan. I don't think he found it too funny at the time, but he laughs about it now. What's even better, Alex scored on the play and I ended up with an assist. I didn't even get a penalty. The referees hadn't seen what happened and I couldn't think of any reason to tell them. I understand that some people might frown on what they consider to be a cheap shot on Stan. To my way of thinking, though, it was just payback. If Stan hadn't touched me, I would have left him alone. I think the rest of the Black Hawks got the message loud and clear as well. If someone took a run at me, he'd better be willing to accept what happened in return.

As younger players like Stan Mikita, Bobby Hull, Jean Béliveau, and Frank Mahovlich came into their own in the early 1960s, I managed to keep myself near the top of the scoring table. It helped to have Sid Abel behind the bench. He took over as coach after Jimmy Skinner stepped aside in 1958. The 1958–59 season was a rough one for the Wings, and it turned out to be the first time in my career that I missed the playoffs. If the experience taught me one thing, it was that sitting at home in the spring wasn't something I wanted to do again. Fortunately, Old Bootnose, as we called Sid, managed to right the ship. His style of hockey suited my game well. By 1961, we were even back in the Stanley Cup finals. We couldn't finish the job, though, and wound up losing to the Black Hawks in six games. Despite that disappointment, a deep playoff run offered some hope for the following season. Our optimism, as it turned out, was misplaced. The 1961–62 season wound up being a dud. For the second time, I found myself on the sidelines watching the postseason as a spectator.

That dismal season turned out to be all she wrote for Jack Adams. Bruce Norris decided that the club needed a change, so after thirty-five years with the Detroit organization, Jack found himself where he'd put so many of his former players—on the street. The general manager's job was given to Sid, who also stayed on behind the bench. I don't think it's the way Mr. Adams envisioned leaving the organization, but it was probably fitting given all the times he'd reminded a departing player that NHL hockey was also a business. Norris did see to it that Mr. Adams landed on his feet after so many years with the club. Following his retirement, the NHL Board of Governors named Mr. Adams as the first president of the Central Professional Hockey League. This was a new league designed to serve as a farm system for the NHL. In its first year, I think it had six teams: Omaha, Indianapolis, St. Louis, Tulsa, Minneapolis, and St. Paul. Mr. Adams was happy to get the job. Although he was sixty-seven years old, I don't think he was ready to step away from the game.

Even without Mr. Adams in the fold, it was still business as usual for the Red Wings at the rink. I had another good year on the score sheet in 1962–63, ending up with 38 goals and 48 assists for 86 points. The tally was good enough for top spot in the league and my sixth Art Ross Trophy. The hockey writers also saw fit to award me my sixth Hart Trophy as the league's most valuable player. I'd also won it in 1951–52, 1952–53, 1956–57, 1957–58, and 1959–60. Both were records that stood until the 1980s, when a young guy named Wayne Gretzky came along and broke them. I had some good years after that season, but it was the last time I won either trophy. By the end of the 1962–63 season, my career goal total stood at 540, only 4 shy of Maurice Richard's all-time record.

Sitting so close to the Rocket's career mark gave me a lot to think about in the off-season. He'd been out of the game for a few years after retiring in the spring of 1960, but I knew he was fiercely proud of his goal-scoring record. Given our history against each other, he couldn't have been happy to see me closing in on that. During our playing days, it would be fair to say that I respected the Rocket but I never liked him. I'm sure he felt the same way about me. It would be lying not to admit that I wanted to take the record away from the Rocket almost as much as I wanted to become the new leader for career goals myself. After I retired, our hard-line stance on each other ended up softening considerably. I couldn't have pictured it when we were battling in the 1950s, but over the years the Rocket and I actually started to see eye to eye. As hard as it might be to imagine, we even became friends.

However, any thoughts of future camaraderie with my former adversary weren't in my head when the season began in 1963. I started off well enough, netting 2 goals in our first game. I added another in our second, which brought me 1 goal shy of the record. I don't know if it was the pressure or what, but with the magic number at 1, the goal-scoring gods decided it was time for a drought. I suffered through the next four games without a goal. It was a long two weeks. I was more than ready to put it behind me by the time the Canadiens came to town on October 27. I generally didn't pay too much attention to the press, but the chatter had become hard to block out. My teammates were feeling it as well. They just wanted me to pot one to get it over with. I finally did us all a favor halfway through the third period. Bill Gadsby sent the puck to Bruce MacGregor, and he passed it to me in the slot. I flicked my wrists like I'd done a million times before and watched the puck sail past Gump Worsley and into the back of the net. The Olympia went nuts. I think the fans wanted me to score worse than I did. They gave me a standing ovation that lasted for a full five minutes. I don't know how many people are lucky enough to experience something like that, but it's a feeling I'll never forget.

As tough as it was to tie the record, breaking it was even harder. Back in 1952–53, when I fell 1 goal shy of equaling Richard's mark of 50 goals, some pundits chalked it up to the pressure of the situation. I can't say I ever agreed with that assessment. Chasing number 545, though, was another story. The pressure was on. I felt it and so did my teammates. As had happened a decade earlier, they started passing up their own chances to score in order to set me up. I appreciated what they were trying to do for me, but I think some of them forgot that we still had games to win. Despite all of their passes, I went dry for another two weeks. It was the longest five-game stretch of my career. It took another visit from the Canadiens to once again break the tension.

Whenever I hit a slump, I tried to get back to thinking just enough but not too much. Hockey moves so fast that you have to react to what's happening in the moment, regardless of whether you had a plan beforehand. I was able to stay in the sweet spot most of the time, which was lucky, because searching for it wasn't fun. Looking back at the chase for number 545, I know now that I was far too deep inside my own head. As the slump went on, I started thinking about all the things I knew about putting the puck in the net. I even thought back to playing goalie as a kid. I remembered that I had the most trouble making saves on low shots. Raising the puck is just doing most goalies a favor. When it's in the air, they can choose to stop it with their body, glove, or blocker. For a shooter, the next best target is high in the corners. When I coached at camps, I'd tell kids to practice taking low, hard shots just above a goalie's ankles, as well as hitting the top corners. Since it had worked for my entire career, it was what I fell back on to break out of my slump. What I wasn't doing at the time, though, was remembering to see what the puck sees. Doing that allows you to simply take what's given to you. That's how I got number 545.

I was killing a power play in the second period when Billy McNeill picked up the puck in our end. He broke out with Bill Gadsby on the left wing and me on the right. As he crossed the Montreal blue line, he slid a pass my way, which I picked up just below the circle. Charlie Hodge was in for Gump that night and I snapped a wrist shot between him and the near post. It went in about hip high. As I was coming in, I saw that Charlie was leaving that space open, so that's what I took. The crowd at the Olympia went crazy once again. They gave me another standing ovation that seemed to last forever. I don't know what felt better: the outpouring of appreciation from thousands of fans or the relief of getting the monkey off my back. Either way, it was a moment I'll never forget. With the big goal out of the way, I also knew my teammates would stop walking on eggshells around me. They'd been treating me like I was a starting pitcher going for a no-hitter. It made for a tight dressing room. After the final buzzer sounded, Henri Richard, the Pocket Rocket, skated over to shake my hand. I'd just broken his brother's record and he wanted to congratulate me. It was a classy gesture.

As it turned out, after that night the record for career goals had my name on it for more than thirty years. By the time my NHL career ended, I'd scored 801 goals, and 68 more in the playoffs. I added another 174 while playing in the World Hockey Association, plus 28 more playoff goals. As much as I enjoyed holding down the top spot, I knew it wouldn't last forever. Records, as they say, are made to be broken. It took until 1994 for mine to fall. Wayne Gretzky, of course, was the one to do it. You don't get called "The Great One" unless you're something special and Wayne, it goes without saying, was a once-in-a-generation talent. Watching his artistry on the ice was a treat for everyone who loves the game of hockey. If anyone had to bump me down the ladder, I'm happy that it was him. As I've always said since then, the way I see it, the record is in good hands.

*Ten*

# TWENTY-FIVE YEARS

When I first made the league as a skinny eighteen-year-old kid, I figured that if I lasted a full season, then for the rest of my life I could say that I had played in the NHL. Once a second season turned into a third, I began to think that a future in hockey was actually realistic. At the ten-year mark, my body was still giving me the green light, so I didn't see any reason to slow down. Even by year thirteen, when the boosters organized Gordie Howe Night, my legs felt like they had a lot of hockey left in them. As the years passed and questions about when I would hang up my skates started to be asked, I still didn't give much thought to retiring. As long as I loved the game, played well enough to help my team, and wasn't cheating the fans, I didn't see any reason to pull up short. Age just seemed like a number. My body had taken care of me through my whole career, so I knew I could also trust it to tell me when it was time to stop.

I'd long thought that twenty years in the league would be a good milestone to reach. By the end of 1966—wouldn't you know it?—I was healthy enough that twenty-five years started to seem reasonable. Not everyone appreciated my patience, I guess. My hometown, for one, got tired of waiting for me to retire before it did something nice. On July 22 of that year, the city of Saskatoon decided to hold a Gordie Howe Day to celebrate my career. Tens of thousands of people showed up to a parade and a rally. They even named a big sports complex after me: Gordon Howe Park. For a kid who got into his share of trouble on those same streets, the idea that I'd one day lead a parade through the town was beyond imagining. At the rally, when they turned the microphone over to me for a few words, it was hard to know what to say. It was a special moment and I had to fight to keep a handle on my emotions. Worried that I might lose the battle, I kept my remarks short. Standing there, looking out over the familiar faces from my hometown, I told the crowd it was something I wouldn't ever get over. All these years later, I can honestly say that I never did.

The celebration that day in Saskatoon also marked the first time in eighteen years I was together with all of my brothers and sisters. Hockey has been so good to me that I don't often say things that might sound like a complaint. I've traveled all over the world. I've played golf with presidents and visited with prime ministers. Hockey even helped me to meet my wife. Despite all of that, though, there have also been some sacrifices, the biggest being my relationships with family. I left home to play in Galt when I was sixteen. Since then, my devotion to the sport and then to Colleen and the kids kept me distant from people I should have kept close. I especially didn't get to know my sisters that well. Sure, I knew them as Gladys, Vi, Joannie, Helen, and Edna, but I didn't know them like you should know family. I didn't know their husbands or their kids. The responsibility for that belongs to me. I wanted to come home more often, but when your career is thousands of miles away it's easier said than done. I remember being back home at a party once with about forty-five people gathered in a room. I didn't recognize many of the faces, so I asked one of my sisters how everyone knew each other. She told me I was related to everyone in the room. I only knew about six of them, but they were all cousins. I wouldn't swap my life for anything, but as the years have passed I've come to understand that playing in the NHL involved trade-offs I wish I hadn't had to make.

The more obvious sacrifice made by every NHL player stares back at you every time you look in the mirror. Your body takes a beating in the big leagues; there's no way around it. I know that today's game is rough on players, but I'm not sure it's rough to the same degree that it was in my day. Modern equipment is light-years ahead of what we strapped on. Our pads were basically glorified cardboard, as opposed to the full-body Kevlar armor that players have now. I actually used to take steps to modify my gear to have it work better. I didn't like anything pulling at my shoulders, so I didn't wear suspenders. Instead, I put on my shoulder pads and just let them lie there. I also used to run a lace through a pair of holes I cut in my pants. I'd tighten it up and then just let my hips hold my pants in position. Pants didn't offer nearly the same protection as they do now. Quick movements would cause you to swivel inside them, which would shift the pads. It exposed your thighs to a lot of charley horses. The manufacturers eventually figured out the problem and started making pants and pads that move with your legs. The innovation has saved players from countless bruises.

Regardless of the advances made with equipment, injuries are still unavoidable. Relatively speaking, though, I don't have much cause to complain. Throughout my career, I was definitely luckier than most when it came to avoiding the big injury. The most time I ever missed in one stretch was in 1948–49, when I sat out twenty games after undergoing knee surgery. Of course, when I do an inventory of my injuries, I can't say that "lucky" is the first word that comes to mind. When a doctor hands me a chart and asks me to mark the places I've been injured, I just draw a line from the top right to the lower left and write in: "All of the above." I can't think of a body part that hasn't been dinged up at some point.

Where to start? I've had teeth knocked out and I've broken all of the usual suspects when it comes to bones: fingers, toes, wrists, feet, and collarbone. The hole they drilled in my skull after the encounter with Teeder Kennedy in 1950—which accompanied a damaged eyeball, broken nose, and fractured cheekbone—is certainly memorable. Not to be left out, my torso has also suffered its share of trauma. One night in Boston, somebody left a gate open and it caught me right on the vulnerable part of the ribs. I had a big lump where the cartilage holds the ribs together. I was so sore that it took a pair of ushers to load me into the cab that took me to the hospital. After getting something to numb the pain, I started to think I could fly home with the guys later that night. That thought lasted only until the freezing wore off and the whole world started to spin. When I made it back on the ice, I had to play with the lump in my ribs for weeks. The other side of my rib cage was spared that time but, just for good measure, I managed to tear it up in a different game. Relative to the gate I hit in Boston, it didn't hurt as much, so I tried to take that as a positive.

I have to admit that often I only had myself to blame for my injuries. I was playing in an exhibition game in Sarnia once when I ran a guy through the double gates of the boards behind the net. One of the gates opened and he went flying out of the rink, but the other side was more stubborn. It stayed shut and caught me right on the collarbone. I was in a lot of pain, but the doctors assured me it was just a sprain. In a different game later on, I took a hit to the same spot and I knew something was off. I went for an X-ray and the doctor told me I'd been playing with a broken collarbone. It was still weak and had become badly bruised after the latest hit. I couldn't believe the doctors in Sarnia saw fit to send me out there with just a pat on the back.

Over my career, I figure I've taken more than 300 stitches to my face alone. Colleen wondered if that might qualify me for a Guinness world record, but I told her I knew some goalies that definitely had me beat. For what it's worth, as a connoisseur on the subject I can tell you that not all stitches are created equal. I labeled the area that ran from my nose to below my mouth as the triangle of pain. Taking stitches there was no kind of fun. Getting sewn up in a place with fewer nerve endings, like the forehead, is a breeze in comparison.

My nose, as you might guess, has also taken a beating over the years. At last count I think it'd been broken fourteen times. Joe Garagiola, the former big league catcher-turned-commentator, once looked at my schnoz and asked how many times I'd broken it. I told him never. "You never did?" he said. "Nope," I replied, "I had fourteen other guys do it for me." It was a line that I like to think would have made Henny Youngman proud.

My poor body also took the business end of a Bobby Hull slap shot more times than I would have liked. He could really shoot the puck. There's an old joke about Bobby and his brother Dennis, whose shot was also heavy but not nearly as accurate as his brother's. The setup went something like this: "Bobby can shoot the puck so hard and fast, he can put it through the entire length of a car wash without getting it wet." Well, went the punch line, "Dennis could do the same thing if he could only hit the car wash." Corny, yes, but it still makes me chuckle. Of course, that joke seemed considerably less funny on the night I took one of Bobby's slap shots to the shin. A few shifts later, I noticed my skate had started to feel sloppy. I thought that too much sweat had run down my leg, so I asked for a change of socks. I also wanted to put the blower into my boot to dry it out. When I peeled off my skate, a half-inch of blood was pooled in it. The famous Hull slap shot had put the puck through my pad and split the skin on my shin right down to the bone. I needed stitches on both the inside and outside of my leg to stop the bleeding.

Another time, I was standing about ten feet to the left of where Bobby should have been aiming when he wound up and let one go. He seemed embarrassed when the puck hit me, putting his hand to his mouth as if to apologize. He wasn't nearly as sorry as I was. The shot was so hard it broke the blade of my skate and the puck fired up into a toe. It hurt like hell. I hobbled over to the bench and pleaded with the trainer, Joe Alcott, to cut off my skate so I could check on my toe, which I knew had to be broken. He told me not to worry since my toe was a long way from my heart. Accepted wisdom of the day suggested that the only injuries considered urgent were ones that involved the heart. I let Joe know exactly what I thought about his medical advice: "My fist is only a foot from your damn nose if you don't start cutting." Naturally, Bobby's errant slap shot had shattered my toe. Joe, of course, was also right. Not much could be done for a broken toe, so I just had to suffer.

Often, the scariest injuries are the ones you can't see. Near the end of my career with Detroit, I ended up suffering a partially detached retina that went undiagnosed. My eyes began to burn and itch and I started to see little spots running through my vision. When I went to see a doctor about it, he told me it was a partial detachment that had started to heal itself. If it started to bleed or I took a good knock to the head, he said I could end up losing my sight. In the course of an average month I took any number of hard hits or collisions, so it was difficult to know the exact cause of this injury. My best guess was an accidental hit I suffered in practice one day. Ned Harkness was our coach at the time and he had us doing a drill where we crisscrossed at the blue line. I thought it was a dumb drill to begin with, since it goes against pretty much everything you're ever taught in hockey, but he was the coach. Partway through the drill, I found myself on a collision course with one of my teammates, so I went to the ice and he tried to jump over me. Of course, he didn't have much of a vertical and he wound up kicking me in the temple. I was immediately woozy. I knew where to find the bench, but when I wobbled over there my eyes couldn't focus. I missed the gate by about three feet and banged into the boards. Lefty Wilson, our trainer, had to come over and help me sit down. After running more tests, the doctor settled on giving me phone numbers for hospitals and specialists in all of the cities we visited on our road trips. If anything funny happened to my vision, I was to call someone immediately. I carried those numbers around with me for a whole year, but thankfully I never had to use them.

As can be expected, playing hockey for a living is also tough on your joints. I banged up my knee so badly one year that I couldn't flex it. They had to go in surgically and scrape off part of my bursa sac to bring down the swelling. My pain tolerance is pretty fair, but that one hurt like a son of a gun. It wasn't the only time I went under the knife for my knees, either. Unfortunately, medicine wasn't as sophisticated as it is now. At the time, if your cartilage was damaged, the surgeon didn't repair it—he just yanked it out. After a few surgeries early in my career, I ended up playing for more than thirty years with no cartilage in either knee. The only thing that saved me was being on the ice instead of on the ground. Skating stresses your knees differently than walking or running does. Playing football or baseball would have worn them out, but hockey kept them somewhat preserved. My original knees actually lasted me until deep into my retirement. I finally went in for some artificial ones when I was around seventy or so, which marked the end of my skating career. The doctors told me if I fell wrong I'd need to have them replaced, and since I'd rather be shot than have to go through that again, I decided it was time to hang up my blades for good. I would have liked to have been able to get on the ice with my great-grandchildren, but I figure my knees granted me enough miles in my life that I owe them the break.

Another injury that stands out was a broken foot I suffered toward the end of my second season in Houston. The pain was manageable, so I kept playing on it until I scored my hundredth point. As soon as that puck went in, I headed off the ice and had a cast put on my foot to get it ready for playoffs. My foot had the last laugh, though. When the season was over, I was told the scorers had made a mistake and I was stuck at 99 points. I figured it was my foot's way of getting back at my ego for having made it suffer. Other injuries, though, are just too painful to play through. I was slashed on the wrists so many times over the years that the bones there were basically reduced to fragments. My radiologist son, Murray, says the X-ray looks like nothing he's ever seen before. He can't believe my wrists let me keep playing hockey for as long as I did. Eventually, though, they didn't. Toward the end of my NHL career, my wrists played a central role in my decision to retire. I was having trouble even gripping the stick with both hands, which basically turned me into a one-handed player. After retiring, my wrists kept hurting so badly I eventually had to give up golf. It's been a real shame. I'd looked forward to playing until a ripe old age, but my hands won't allow me to grip a club well enough to swing it. I can roll some balls on the putting green, but I can't get out for a round.

Oddly enough, the worst pain I ever felt didn't come from playing hockey. We were on the road when I woke up with an attack of kidney stones. The pain was agonizing. By the next morning, I looked like a dead horse. I managed to endure the trip back to Detroit, but once I got home the pain became so severe it scared me. Our daughter, Cathy, heard me moaning and ran to our room to see what was wrong. She saw me lying in the fetal position in my bathrobe and started to cry. My legs were curled up and she thought they'd fallen off. Poor girl. Colleen managed to bundle me into the car and we headed for the hospital. Of course, Murphy's Law kicked in and it was rush hour. Colleen ducked out of gridlock and picked her way through side streets all the way to the hospital. Once we arrived, they gave me something for the pain, which knocked me out, gratefully. I ended up passing the stone during the night. It had to be the size of a golf ball. The next morning Colleen showed up with pajamas and my shaving kit, figuring I'd need them over the next few days in the hospital. With the kidney stone gone, I not only felt well enough to go home but also didn't see any reason why I shouldn't play in our game that night. Colleen thought the decision was asinine. She always had a way with words when we argued. I won out, though, and made it onto the ice that night with my teammates. I actually played pretty well, notching a goal and an assist through two periods. Eventually, the pain and exhaustion of the previous few days caught up with me, and I sat down for the third period. I figured it was a good compromise.

In the NHL, playing through pain should be part of the job description. If you can't do it, you'll barely ever make it onto the ice. A reporter once asked me how many times I'd been hurt in my career. I told him that I'd been hurt in some way or another in every game I'd ever played. As a professional athlete, it's critical to be able to distinguish between being hurt and being injured. Hurt you can play through, but if you're injured you'd better sit down or risk making it worse. I always tried to be honest with myself, but if I had any say in the matter I wanted to be there for my teammates. I knew that I couldn't do anything to help them in street clothes, so if I could pull on my gear I wanted to give it a shot. Teammates aside, players in my era didn't need much of a push to play. A lack of job security did wonders for our collective pain tolerance. Whether it was a broken bone or a 102-degree fever, thoughts of next season's salary acted as a pretty effective tonic. You didn't feel too good about sitting down, knowing that your spot in the league depended on you being on the ice and not on the bench.

Although my career lasted for thirty-two years, my laundry list of injuries offered a constant reminder that I couldn't play forever. In the late 1950s, our family was lucky enough to take some big steps toward securing our finances away from the game. Oddly enough, it was someone's business decision to reject me as a client that opened a lot of other doors. After an offer to do some promotional work came in from the T. Eaton Company, the biggest retailer in Canada at the time, we went looking for a manager to handle the deal. Someone suggested a bright young guy named Mark McCormack, who went on to found IMG, one of the world's biggest management companies. At the time, he was just starting out and had only one client. He was a biggie, though: Arnold Palmer. With Arnie in the fold, McCormack said he was too busy to take me on as well. He ended up doing us a favor. After his rejection, we wondered who could do a better job of looking out for the family's business interests than Colleen? She turned out to be a natural. Muhammad Ali, of all people, even nicknamed her "The Boss." Her appointment calendar, which she treated like another child, helped us keep a lot of balls in the air over the years. Along with Eaton's, we were lucky enough to establish good relationships with companies such as Lincoln-Mercury, Emery Worldwide, Neilson Chocolate, Zellers, Rayovac, Bank of Nova Scotia, and Quaker State. We also teamed up with some friends to open Gordie Howe Hockeyland, a big indoor ice-skating complex in St. Clair Shores, a town just northeast of Detroit. In the 1960s, kids came from all over Michigan and Canada to skate there twelve months a year. It still makes me proud to think that we helped to bring the game to a generation of kids who grew up playing there.

While the endorsement deals and our other business interests helped our family's bottom line, my main source of income was always hockey. Even after Jack Adams left, the club continued to assure me that I was among the highest-paid players in the game. It took until the late 1960s before I found out otherwise. By that time, not only was my body starting to fray around the edges but my relationship with the Wings was showing some wear and tear as well.

The credit for opening my eyes to what was happening around the league belongs to Bobby Baun. He's best remembered as a

Maple Leaf, but when Toronto didn't protect him ahead of the 1967 expansion draft he was selected by the Oakland Seals and spent a miserable year playing on the west coast. After finishing dead last overall, Oakland accommodated Bobby's trade request and dealt him to Detroit before the 1968–69 season. As it happened, Bobby was one of the first presidents of the new NHL Players' Association that started in the late 1960s. He was also one of the few players to flout the owners' rules about sharing details of his salary. His straight talk with players on every team gave him a good idea of what everyone was making and what we were worth.

In those years, Detroit held its training camp in Port Huron. We were out for dinner one night when Bobby looked over and called me a stupid SOB. I told him I had reasons enough of my own to agree with that statement, but I wanted to know his. He told me I'd been undervaluing my services for years. Even *his* salary, he said, was bigger than mine. I didn't think he knew what he was talking about, so I asked him how much he thought I was making. My salary was around $45,000 at the time and he pegged it nearly exactly. Not only were other guys in the league making more money than me, but I wasn't even the highest-paid player on my own team. I later found out that Carl Brewer, another of our defensemen, had also signed a much bigger deal than mine. That made me steaming mad. Clearly, this had been going on for years, meaning I'd left Lord only knows how much money on the table. I talked to Bruce Norris and asked that my salary be raised to $100,000. When he agreed to it straightaway, I immediately knew that everything Bobby was telling me was on the mark. In retrospect, I should have asked for $150,000. I don't like to think about how much my family lost out on over the years because of the trust I put in management. It was more than just the money, however; I felt betrayed. The team liked to talk about how the organization was like a family, but in that moment it sure didn't feel like it.

As the 1960s were coming to a close, the Red Wings were struggling through a series of tough seasons. After losing to the Canadiens in the Stanley Cup finals in 1966, we hit a drought that would have been unthinkable during the glory years of the 1950s. In the five seasons between 1966 and 1971, we only made the playoffs once, in 1970. Even that was a short trip, with Chicago sweeping us in the quarterfinals. The next season we were back in the gutter, managing a paltry 22 wins and 11 ties. Our seventh-place finish once again put us out of the playoffs.

At forty-three years old, I was starting to feel my age on the ice for the first time in my life. My injuries were taking longer to heal and my legs didn't have their usual jump. In twenty-five years with the Red Wings, hardly a day had gone by that I hadn't looked forward to coming to the arena. That season, the fire that I had always taken for granted started to burn lower. By then, my time in the league had been a long haul any way you wanted to slice it. In the 1950s, I'd missed a total of twelve games due to injury, six in 1954–55 and another six in 1957–58. I'd missed even fewer games in the 1960s. My body had seen a lot of hockey over two decades in the NHL and it was starting to talk to me pretty loudly. Even carrying my stick was becoming tough, due to the chronic arthritis in my wrists. I had surgery to clean up some bone fragments, but it only helped so much. The 1970–71 season counts among the worst of my career. I lost ten games to a rib injury and was hampered by one injury or another for the rest of the year. I just couldn't seem to get on track. I ended up with 23 goals and 29 assists for 52 points, my lowest total since my injury-shortened season in 1948–49.

By the time the off-season came around, retirement had become a serious consideration. When Guy Lafleur hung up his skates in the 1980s, I remember talking to him about a comeback. I advised him not to quit as long as he had some music left in him. If he knew he was done, then fine, but if he had any doubts he owed it to himself to get back on the ice. Well, in 1971, I was having a hard time hearing the music. The organization was in shambles, the team was losing, and our prospects for the next season weren't looking any better. A few years earlier I would have had a lot to say about that, but injuries and age had me wondering how much I could still help the club. According to Colleen, if my performance was up to my own standards and I thought I was still doing right by the fans, then I should keep playing. She just didn't want to see me suffer through another year of being disappointed in myself. Hockey was all I'd ever wanted to do and all I'd ever known, but when I looked at myself in the mirror that summer, I realized it might be time for a change. After several long months of deliberation, I announced my retirement in early September. It was a difficult moment. For the first time in a quarter-century, when the puck dropped to start the next season, I wouldn't be a part of it.

*Eleven*

# HEADING TO HOUSTON

Nobody teaches an athlete how to retire. I wish I could say that adjusting to civilian life was easy, but it wasn't. Every job comes with its own rhythms—when you wake up, what you eat, where you go to work, who you see there—and the NHL is no different. For twenty-five years, my life was regulated by the changing seasons. Training camp in the fall became the regular season during the winter, which melted into springtime and the playoffs. A summer of family and rest followed (with a lake nearby if we were lucky). As the 1971–72 NHL season began, all sorts of changes were coming my way, but at the very least I still had hockey in my life. The Red Wings had assured me I'd always have a job with the club and they made good on those promises, announcing after my retirement that I'd joined the front office. There was also talk of learning the insurance game and stepping into an executive role at one of the Norris family's companies. It was a new world, but it seemed promising. At forty-three, I was old for a hockey player, but I figured I was just entering my prime by most other standards. I planned to treat my new job the same as I had my old one. I might have traded skates and shoulder pads for a shirt and tie, but when I stepped into the Olympia I was still ready to put in a hard day's work. Unfortunately, not everyone got the memo.

After our early discussions about the job, I came away assuming I'd have a role in shaping the on-ice product. It only made sense, given my knowledge of the game and my experience with the team, but it didn't turn out to be the case. The Red Wings, it seemed, didn't know what to do with me. Instead of involving me in team decisions, they parked me in a tiny office and dusted me off only when it was time to make a public appearance. Officially, I was eventually given the title of vice president of public relations. In practice, I was more like vice president of an empty desk. The team was paying me $50,000 a year to sit around. For someone who'd been working since he was a kid, it was the first time in my life I didn't feel like I was earning my paycheck. As much as I tried to change things, it felt like the club only wanted me around as a hood ornament. It wasn't a good feeling.

My duties were largely limited to representing the Red Wings at banquets and functions. I don't mind eating a rubber-chicken dinner every now and then, but I knew I had more to offer. However, my attempts to get something going often led to a promise that someone would get back to me in a couple of days. Of course, when the time came, nothing ever materialized. In hindsight, the writing on the wall was pretty clear. The club didn't have a real place for me and neither did anyone in the insurance business. Regardless of the lip service, no one on either side was interested in taking the time to carve out a space for me. One time, I went to a banquet in suburban Detroit, where I was told I'd be joining other members of the club. I arrived to a packed house but found myself alone at a ten-person table designated for the Red Wings. I waited around for a while, until it became clear that no one else was going to show. I was about to leave when one of the organizers stopped me and said I was getting an award that night. The team hadn't even bothered to let me know that I was one of the guests of honor. The poor guy had to round up eight other people to sit at the table with me. On the drive home, I thought about how the lack of consideration was pretty typical of my new job. (At one of those banquets, in Brantford, I did get the chance to meet an eleven-year-old Wayne Gretzky. He was just a skinny little guy with a big smile, but he was already a phenom. We bonded right away. Little did I know that a few years later I'd be looking up at him in the record books.)

It was a frustrating time made all the worse by a tremendous personal loss that my family had just suffered. The summer before, as I was contemplating my retirement, my mother passed away after falling at our cabin in northern Michigan. Colleen and I were at an event in Toronto when it happened. We'd left the kids with Mum and Dad at the cabin for a few days. My mother was a kind, generous, warmhearted person, and I loved her dearly. I still miss her to this day. I announced my retirement a few weeks later.

As much as I would have liked to throw myself into something as a distraction, my new career didn't turn out to be the thing. I don't doubt that the club had good intentions, at least in the beginning. Bruce Norris definitely seemed to want me to be part of the organization, but his people were another matter. If someone doesn't consider you essential, they'll find ways to put you on the sidelines. I call it the mushroom treatment. You're kept in the dark and every now and then they come in and throw a little manure on you. The office they stuck me in told the whole story. It was so shabby that the club moved me to better digs when it needed to take a promotional picture. When I showed up in front-office shots, Colleen and I would always laugh because the pictures in the background were of someone else's family.

With so much time on my hands, I started thinking about an old dream I had of staying in the game long enough to play with my kids. I'd had a little taste of it during a charity match in my final year with the Red Wings, and I'd loved how good it made me feel. Years earlier, Colleen had become involved with the Junior Red Wings program, a successful junior rep team that played out of the Olympia. In 1971, Marty, at sixteen, and Mark, at fifteen, were both playing for the squad when Colleen organized a fund-raiser for the March of Dimes that pitted the junior team against the parent club. I suited up for the young guys along with my older brother Vern, who'd played a few games for the Rangers in the 1950s. The Olympia was packed and the fans were having a great time. It was a real Howe family affair. With the score tied 10–10, we even got Murray into the action. He was only about ten years old at the time, but he was already a good little player. We cut a deal with the opposing goalie and, with about five seconds left in the game, Murray walked in and scored. The crowd loved it. My favorite part of the night was hearing the announcer tell the crowd that the goal had been scored by "Howe from Howe and Howe." I thought it would be the only time I'd get the chance to hear that line uttered. I couldn't know how wrong I'd turn out to be.

By 1972–73, Marty and Mark had both moved on from the Junior Red Wings to play for the Toronto Marlboros of the Ontario Hockey League. Marty had arrived there a year earlier and was excited for his brother to join him. At that point, both of my sons were considered solid prospects. Mark was even picked to play on the U.S. Olympic team that won a silver medal in the 1972 Winter Games in Sapporo, Japan. At sixteen, I think he's still the youngest player to ever win an Olympic medal in hockey. The following year, he was named MVP of the Memorial Cup when he and Marty helped lead the Marlies to Canada's junior hockey national championship. I felt proud that both of my sons appeared to have a legitimate future in professional hockey. The rules at the time, though, meant they'd have to wait. The NHL didn't allow junior players to be drafted until after they turned twenty. That meant Marty would have to spend one more year in Toronto before he could be drafted and Mark would have to wait another two. At that point, fate intervened in a way we hadn't expected.

Colleen and I, dressed to the nines, were on our way out the door to an art auction to benefit the Arthritis Foundation when the phone rang. When I picked it up, Doug Harvey, of all people, was on the other end of the line. My old adversary from the Montreal Canadiens was now an assistant coach with the Houston Aeros, a new team in the World Hockey Association, an upstart league that was becoming a big thorn in the side of the NHL. Doug told me the Aeros were getting ready to walk into the WHA meetings and draft Mark with their first-round pick. He wanted to give me a heads-up, because when it happened he knew all hell would break loose and the press was sure to be calling. Not long after that, Bill Dineen, the head coach of the Aeros and a former teammate in Detroit, stood up and said, "Houston drafts Mark Howe," a sentence that sent a shock wave through the entire hockey world.

Mark was still only eighteen, and the other teams in the WHA had assumed that their league would abide by the same rules as the NHL. Houston was ready to gamble that an age restriction was illegal and wouldn't hold up against a court challenge. I suspect the other teams were upset only because they hadn't thought of it first. It was a bold stroke by the Aeros, and perfectly in line with the spirit of the league. When the WHA started in 1972–73, it was the first direct competitor the NHL had seen in decades. It was born out of the idea that North America's appetite for hockey had room for more than just the NHL. The twelve-team WHA included cities without an NHL franchise, such as Winnipeg, Ottawa, and Cleveland, as well as bigger centers with populations that could support multiple teams, such as New York and Los Angeles.

For the most part, the new league was populated with career minor-leaguers, NHL journeymen, college players, and eventually even Europeans, who were rare in the NHL at the time. To gain credibility, the WHA also pushed to lure big-name NHL stars away from their current clubs. Looking to make a splash, the new owners dangled higher salaries in front of players who had been underpaid for years. To the consternation of their NHL masters, Derek Sanderson, Mike Walton, Pat Stapleton, Dave Keon, and Bernie Parent were among those to make the switch. The new league even took a run at Bobby Orr, arguably the biggest star in the NHL. By far the biggest get, though, was a pretty big star himself: Bobby Hull. The Golden Jet became a real-life Jet, leaving Chicago to take over as player–coach in Winnipeg. The competition from the WHA did more than annoy the NHL; it also caused salaries to start escalating across the board. The players were happy, but it actually backfired on the fledgling league, which was financially unsteady from the start. Team finances aside, the WHA offered another opportunity for hockey players to make a living. Still only teenagers, Mark and Marty couldn't believe they might not have to put their professional dreams on hold any longer.

Colleen and I would have loved to be at the draft in Winnipeg when the Aeros called Mark's name. When we finally made it to the auction that night, it's safe to say our minds weren't on the art. As it turned out, Houston wasn't done dropping bombs on the league and our family. With their twelfth-round pick, they selected Marty. Both picks were a big gamble for the club at the time. If they were wrong about the legality of drafting underage players, the team would have squandered a pair of valuable picks. If it hadn't before, the new league had now definitely captured the NHL's attention. By snatching up the best young players from the junior ranks, the WHA threatened to upset the balance of power in the hockey world. The NHL was worried enough that, the next day, I got a call from no less than Clarence Campbell himself. The NHL's president spoke to me at length about the ramifications of our boys playing for the Aeros. It would be a heavy blow to the league, he said, as well as something that would potentially jeopardize the entire system of junior hockey. He ended by imploring me to forbid my boys from signing with Houston.

After I hung up the phone, I spent the rest of the day full of mixed emotions. The NHL had been a fixture in my life for more than a quarter-century. I owed the league so much that I didn't even want to think about the possibility of turning my back on it. Added to which, I never thought it was good business to bite the hand that feeds you. That said, I thought back to my dad telling us kids that if you didn't look out for yourself, no one else would. In the end, our decision came down to doing what we thought was best for our boys. I called Mr. Campbell back the next day and told him that I couldn't ask Mark and Marty to deny themselves an opportunity they'd worked so hard to earn. I wouldn't have wanted my father to ask it of me, and I wasn't going to ask it of them. The decision, I told him, would be theirs to make.

For Houston, the move to draft underage players wasn't a gimmick. They'd scouted Mark and Marty all year and figured our boys had enough talent to make a difference on the ice. To succeed as a league, the WHA clubs knew they needed to build teams around good young players. Our kids were just the first. As far as Bill Dineen and Doug Harvey were concerned, the hockey side of the business mattered more than having a famous last name. As for me, I'd harbored the dream of our boys playing professional hockey for as long as I could remember.

The thought was even on my mind on the night the Red Wings retired my jersey. The club held a big ceremony between periods of a game against the Black Hawks in the spring of 1972. A carpet emblazoned with a big number 9 was rolled out and I was joined on the ice by Colleen and all of our kids except Marty, who had a junior game in Toronto that night. It was an elaborate deal. U.S. Vice President Spiro Agnew even showed up at the behest of President Nixon. When I accepted the honor from Bruce Norris, my only request was that the sweater would be made available if one of my boys ever played with the club. Mark, who's now a scout with the Red Wings, eventually did just that at the end of his career, but he chose to wear number 4 instead. Of course, he's best remembered for the number 2 he wore in Philadelphia. The Flyers put that sweater in the rafters a few years ago, making Mark only the fifth player in franchise history to receive that honor.

Shortly after the WHA draft, we called the boys and brought them home to Detroit. The rest of the hockey world might have had a tough time dealing with the idea of them turning professional, but they didn't share those concerns. The thought of getting paid for something they'd been doing for free for so long was all the convincing they needed. Colleen and I figured we could do more than just give them our blessing. Once their decision was made, we turned our attention to cutting the best deal possible for our boys. I'd spent nearly my whole career earning less than market value and we were determined the same thing wouldn't happen to them.

As the flap about the underage rule continued, I was logging a lot of time on the phone with Bill Dineen, who was keeping us updated on how things were unfolding on the legal end. The Aeros looked to have a good case, but once lawyers get involved everything becomes a much longer slog. During one of our conversations I finally dropped an idea on Bill that had been spinning in my head since the whole thing had started. I asked him what he thought of three Howes playing in Houston. There was a long pause before he asked me if I was serious. I told him I was. In that case, he told us, Colleen and I should start making plans to visit Texas.

While only a few weeks earlier I had been grinding away unhappily behind a desk at the Olympia, the idea of a comeback suddenly became real in a hurry. When I'd hung up my skates, I'd assumed I was done for good. Two years on, though, the wrist problems that had played such a big role in my decision to retire seemed to be less of an issue. Over time, the surgeries to remove the bone fragments had started to bring more feeling back to my hands. My wrists weren't exactly healed—they were still sore and my arthritis hadn't gone away—but my time away from the game had given the joints time to recover.

The idea of my returning to the ice made Colleen apprehensive from the start. At forty-five, I'd be playing against kids half my age. I also had a list of injuries as long as my arm and I hadn't played a serious game of hockey in two years. I won't say I didn't share her concerns, but I told her I always knew what I was capable of when it came to hockey. I'd have to get back into game shape, but I rarely struggled with conditioning. All of the miles I'd skated on choppy outdoor ice in Saskatoon had built a lifetime of strength into my legs. I knew they'd be there for me if I asked. The bigger issue would come from deeper inside. When I retired in 1971, my heart wasn't in the game the way it needed to be. After two unhappy years away from the ice, though, I'd come to realize something crucial about myself. I was a hockey player, first, last, and always. The thought of lacing them up in Houston to play alongside my boys made me feel like I was twenty-two again. I couldn't wait to get back on the ice.

However, before any of the Howes pulled on an Aeros jersey, we still had to take care of the business end of the deal. We invited Doug Harvey, Bill and Pat Dineen, and Houston's team president, Jim Smith, up to our cabin at Bear Lake. The first thing we wanted to sort out was whether the money would be right for both parties. If the dollars didn't make sense, there wouldn't be much point in going any further. We also wanted to get a better feel for the organization and the city of Houston. After twenty-seven years with one club, I knew all too well how big of a say the front office had in your overall happiness. The delegation from Houston ended up checking all the boxes. By the end of their visit, we'd worked out a package deal for the three of us. It would be worth nearly $2.5 million over four years. Negotiating the contract made me think back to my first year in Omaha. I'd earned $2700 in 1945 and felt like I was king of the world. After taking less than market value for so many years, the Houston deal finally gave our family the long-term financial security I had wanted during my whole career. I liked the contract as a hockey player, but I loved it as a father and a husband.

Following our retreat to Bear Lake, our due diligence continued with a trip to Houston. Before we uprooted our kids from their home, we wanted to meet the owners of this new hockey club and make sure they could deliver on their promises. When the plane touched down, it marked Colleen's first time in Texas. The Aeros met us at the airport with a limousine and placed yellow roses in our suite, which had a personalized nameplate affixed to the door. That night we took in a baseball game with the owners and their wives at the Astrodome. No papers had been signed yet, but the visit went a long way toward alleviating any lingering doubts. The money was right, we liked the city, and the organization looked to be filled with people of substance. By that point, we'd whittled down our checklist to two outstanding items: a conversation with Cathy and Murray, and another with Bruce Norris. Neither would be easy.

Only five weeks had passed since Doug Harvey's draft-night phone call, but they'd flown by in a blur. Although our minds were made up about Houston, I was hesitant to tell the Wings. Despite all of our recent ups and downs, the team was still the only employer I'd known in my adult life. I hadn't had much more than the clothes on my back when Jack Adams signed me to my first deal. Hockey and the Red Wings had given me a life. Saying good-bye wasn't going to be easy. Houston had agreed to let me handle my business in Detroit before saying anything about our deal. They had the press release ready to go; all they needed was my okay. Keeping it under wraps wasn't easy. The press could sense something in the air, and it was starting to swarm. Colleen started to press me to tell the Wings to put an end to the circus. It was something that had to be done in my own time, though. I let a few more days pass before finally picking up the phone and calling Bruce.

In the eleven years between 1966 and 1977, the Red Wings suffered through the worst stretch in team history, appearing in the playoffs only once, in 1970. They snapped the dry spell in 1978, but after a quarterfinals loss to Montreal it took another six years for the team to see the postseason again. All of the losing tested the patience of a loyal fan base, which wanted nothing more than to see the club put a winner on the ice. I knew that my phone call to Bruce in June 1973 wouldn't help matters. When I reached him at his office at the Olympia, our conversation was short and to the point. I told him I hadn't signed with Houston yet, but I'd made up my mind and I wouldn't be returning to the club. He said he was sorry the situation had turned out the way it did. I agreed.

When I announced my resignation later that night, I tried to speak honestly about my situation. I told the press that the last few years hadn't been happy ones for me and I was considering an offer from Houston, where I could play with my sons. The Detroit papers took it easy on me, but they used the opportunity to unload on the organization. As a loyal and longtime employee of the club, it wasn't how I wanted to leave. Unfortunately, the acrimony ended up taking on a life of its own. When the team handed over my last paycheck, it was for the princely sum of $51. Normally it ran around $2000, but the team had decided to deduct my recent travel expenses. We booked all of our travel, both personal and business, through the Olympia Travel Bureau, which Bruce Norris owned. We always settled up our account promptly, but with me on the way out the door, they apparently wanted to make sure I didn't skip town owing them any money. After twenty-seven years of faithful service, being considered a deadbeat felt like an unnecessary slap in the face.

My love for the Red Wings meant that I'd hoped to leave the club on good terms, but sports doesn't always work out that way. The nature of the job as an athlete is different than trading stocks or crunching numbers. Players and teams often have relationships that are very public and deeply personal. It's why even stoic athletes will tear up when announcing that they're switching teams or retiring. I never considered my relationship with the Red Wings to be just about business. It might have drifted in that direction toward the end, but it's still not how I feel about the team.

Just as hard as leaving the organization was saying good-bye to Detroit. By then, I'd lived there nearly twice as long as I had in Saskatoon. It was where Colleen and I had met and it was the only home our kids had ever known. The first house we bought after we were married was on Stawell Avenue. It was about three miles west of the Olympia and not far from where Colleen grew up. Marty and Mark were both born while we lived there. As they grew we started to feel like we needed more space, so we moved north to Lathrup Village. We had Cathy and Murray while in that house. All of our kids grew up skating on the ice rink we built in the front yard. Once I retired we bought a bigger house in Bloomfield Hills, an uptown suburb even farther north of the city.

When the time came to move to Houston, we had a tough decision to make about Murray. At thirteen, he was coming into his own on the ice and living in Texas, where the minor hockey system wasn't close to what it was in Michigan, would have killed his chances to follow in his brothers' footsteps. We'd always given our children a lot of room to make their own decisions, so we left the choice up to him. It wasn't easy on the family, but he decided he loved hockey too much to give it up. To our relief, some good friends, the Robertsons, generously offered to take him in. They had five kids of their own and Murray had grown up around their house. Murray was our youngest and leaving him in Detroit was hard, but it's what he wanted. I didn't tell him so at the time, but I knew I would have done the same thing if I'd been in his shoes.

What seemed unthinkable only a few months earlier had quickly become a reality. The Howe family had a plan: Murray would stay in Bloomfield Hills and chase his hockey dreams. The rest of us, meanwhile, would head to Texas to follow our own.

*Twelve*

# OVERTIME

T he Howe family is full of great runners. My dad could run like a deer. Cathy ran track in high school. Murray has completed marathons and Colleen even ran a road race once. Running comes much less naturally to Mark and me. Just a few steps into a jog and my legs begin to feel like they're plodding up and down like an elephant's. Ideally, I prefer to do my conditioning on the ice or even on a stationary bike if necessary. Sometimes, though, you just need to bite the bullet. Once we landed in Houston, I knew I was serious about getting in shape when I added roadwork to my training regimen. My logic was the same as that of a kid who doesn't like brussels sprouts. Anything I hated that much, I figured, had to be good for me.

Spending a couple of years eating banquet food and sitting behind a desk hadn't done much for my waistline. I hadn't let myself go entirely, but at 223 pounds I was twelve or fourteen pounds over where I thought my playing weight should be. Colleen posted my weight on the refrigerator in bold numbers to remind me about the task at hand. Once I committed to getting back in shape, my body felt like the engine of an old rust bucket in the middle of a Detroit winter. It took a long time to turn over. In the beginning I'd take a hundred strides, walk to recover, and then run again. I gradually built up to running for two hundred steps, and then three hundred. I finally reached the point where I could run the whole thing and still have enough gas left in the tank to sprint to the end. The last fifty yards of my circuit were dead uphill, so the finishing kick always brought some pain. It was worth it, though. Between running, lifting weights, and riding a bike, I was starting to feel more like my old self. Regardless of what happened on land, though, I knew the bigger test was still to come.

Watching me huff and puff my way through the first few practices, the Aeros probably wondered if they'd made a very expensive mistake. There's no way to sugarcoat it: I was terrible. I was sucking wind during drills and scrimmages like I never had before. Marty later told me that my face turned a shade of red and purple that had him a bit worried. I'm sure my new teammates thought the old man would give up the ghost before he ever saw a shift. I didn't know it at the time, but my sons were so concerned they started calling Colleen at home to keep her updated. A doctor had given me a clean bill of health before we went to Houston, but it hadn't done much to alleviate her worries. My struggles only confirmed her suspicion that she would have to try to talk me out of the whole idea before the season started. Just as the storm clouds were looking darkest, Bill Dineen piled on by telling us that training camp was moving to two practices a day. It was the only time I truly questioned my decision to go to Houston. When Colleen and I talked that night, I admitted that there was a chance our WHA adventure could end badly. Just like always, however, she told me the only thing to do was to put one foot in front of the other and see where it went. In this case, it was actually one skate in front of the other, but I got the point. I figured that two-a-days would either cure me or kill me. My body was so exhausted by that point, I'm not sure which one I was hoping for more.

They say it's always darkest before the dawn, and sometimes they're actually right. A few days later my body didn't hurt quite so much. Practice that day was also different. Before, my legs had been heavy, but now they were starting to get some of their old jump back. I began to feel good, like I'd been skating all year. The imaginary piano that had been strapped to my back also disappeared, thankfully. I still had a lot of work to do, but it was as if I'd broken through an invisible wall. The doubts were gone. Hockey was hockey again, and I knew I'd be okay.

From the outside looking in, it might have appeared that the Howe family circus in Houston was just a novelty act cooked up by the WHA to sell tickets. Admittedly, the script looked like something out of a bad movie. An over-the-hill former star was coming out of retirement to play ice hockey in Texas with his two teenage sons. It was no gimmick, though. I'd never played in a game where there was a chance of embarrassing myself, and I didn't intend to start. As for my boys, they were the real deal. Some reporters suggested that Marty and Mark snuck into the league on the coattails of my comeback, but that couldn't have been further from the truth. If anything, I was tagging along with them. I was just a short-timer, but they were the future.

We knew that any publicity we could bring to the WHA would help the cause. Texans love their sports, but they hadn't had much experience with hockey. We were game for anything we could do to promote the team. Well, almost anything. I drew the line at elephants. A year earlier, Bill Dineen had volunteered to ride an elephant in Houston's Shrine Circus parade. He was busy waving to the crowd when the elephant in front of his decided to empty its bladder. Before Bill knew what was happening, his elephant dipped its trunk in the puddle, slurped up the pool of liquid, and proceeded to spray it all over its rider. I loved hockey, but I didn't know if I loved it as much as Bill. Elephants aside, our preseason tour was full of newspaper interviews, talk shows, and radio spots. Everyone wanted to know how the old man would fare once he got on the ice. I have to admit, I did too.

The city of Houston, for its part, was behind us from the start. On the way to the arena for the home opener, we looked up and saw a big banner hanging from one of the office towers. It read: "Welcome to Howeston." I just hoped I could live up to my end of the deal. I'd wrenched my back during our exhibition tour and it was still acting up by game day. I'd spent the previous night in traction at the hospital trying to get it ready. Colleen wanted me to sit out the opener, but I figured I owed it to myself, and to the Aeros, to give it a try.

Skating onto the ice for the first time in Houston was surreal. After spending a quarter-century wearing red and white in Detroit, I hardly recognized myself when I looked down and saw blue for the first time. (It reminded me of a bad dream I had once, in which Trader Jack dealt me to the Leafs.) Sam Houston Coliseum had taken the place of the Olympia. It wasn't a bad old barn, but it had seen better days. By the time the puck dropped, about two-thirds of its roughly nine thousand–seat capacity was full. Our trainer, Bobby Brown, had his hands full keeping my back spasms at bay. Every time I came off the ice, he hooked me up to a little black box with a wire that sent an electric pulse into my back. The thing worked like a charm. I played the whole game, but it still wasn't enough to get the season off on the right foot and we ended up losing to the Cleveland Crusaders. On the way off the ice, a funny thing happened. The fans cheered for us like we'd just skated the other guys out of the building. Mark, who always took losses hard, didn't know what to make of it. I told him they just appreciated our effort. They cheered everything, the good plays as well as the bad. They even cheered the ice-sweeping crew. Looking back, I think the fans knew they'd eventually figure out the hockey part and, in the meantime, they weren't going to let any of the details spoil a good time.

It didn't take the team long to start repaying the fans for their loyalty. Bill had put together a nice little squad. Not only were we good once the puck dropped but also our camaraderie off the ice turned out to be special. Our roster might have been bookended by the oldest player in the league and the youngest, but it didn't matter; all of us were pulling in the same direction. It brought back memories of my early days in Detroit. None of us was making much money at the time, so when we'd go out on the town Alex Delvecchio would get everyone to throw $5 on the table. When the pile was gone, the drinkers would put down more money and whoever was done could leave gracefully. If you wanted only a beer or two, it meant you weren't stuck buying rounds for the whole squad the entire night. Little things like that matter to team chemistry. For some guys, it can make the difference between hanging out with teammates or spending time alone. In Houston, we had guys looking out for the little things. With so many of us new to town, the team ended up doing everything together. As so often happens with close-knit groups, the results started to show on the ice.

By the time I reached Houston, I hadn't won a championship in nearly twenty years. My final seasons in Detroit had been so grim that the notion of winning anything substantial hadn't even crossed my mind for a while. Retiring then put an end to the idea altogether. At forty-five years old, who would have thought I'd get another chance, and in Texas of all places? Our 48 wins and 5 ties put us on top of our division. During the season both Mark and Marty proved that Houston's decision to draft underage players was based on sound hockey logic. Mark was named rookie of the year and Marty established himself as a defenseman the league would have to reckon with for a long time to come. As for me, I think I might have surprised a few people, maybe even myself. I had a private goal of 70 points, but I hadn't counted on the team gelling as it did or the arthritis in my wrists easing off enough to allow me to start feeling the puck again. With 31 goals and 69 assists for an even 100 points, I was named the league's most valuable player. What's even better, the team kept winning in the playoffs, beating Winnipeg in the quarterfinals and Minnesota in the semis to earn our way to the finals.

The WHA didn't miss many tricks when it came to earning a few extra dollars. Looking for any way it could to bring in some money, it sold the naming rights to its championship trophy to a defense contractor called Avco. The big prize in the league was thereafter known as the Avco Cup. It lacked the history of the Stanley Cup and it was certainly more commercial, but everything has to start somewhere. Like any team fighting for a championship, we'd put a lot of blood, sweat, and tears into the season and we wanted to take home the trophy, regardless of what it was called. The finals couldn't have gone any better. We played the Chicago Cougars and swept them in four straight to win the second title in the WHA's brief history. I hadn't tasted champagne in the dressing room since 1955. It was just as sweet as I remembered.

When we sat down with Jim Smith and Bill Dineen to broker our contract with the Aeros, only the first year of my deal was set in stone. At the time, I hadn't been certain if my body would hold up or how I'd feel about the rigors of practice and the grind of being on the road. As ever, winning a title did wonders for my aches and pains. Playing in front of full houses in Houston alongside my boys was also so much fun that I had a big decision to make about whether I had more hockey left in me. I'd put in enough work to get back in shape that I figured my forty-six-year-old bones could handle another year if I asked them to. The lure of playing against the Russians was also tempting.

The powers that be had organized another Summit Series between Canada and the U.S.S.R., to be held before the start of the next season. Along with every other Canadian, I'd watched in 1972 as our national team beat the Soviets in what became an instant classic. This time around, a team of WHA all-stars would be representing Canada. The thought of wearing the Maple Leaf was too good to pass up. I was picked for the team along with Marty and Mark. Bobby Hull was on the squad, as well as Frank Mahovlich, Paul Henderson, and Pat Stapleton. They'd all played in the 1972 series and did their best to brace us for what to expect.

Unfortunately, we didn't fare as well as they had. We ended the series with one win, four losses, and three ties. I don't have many regrets when it comes to hockey, but I do wish I could have played against the Russians when I was ten years younger. Facing them with fewer miles on my legs and more jump in my step would have been interesting.

When we landed back in Houston for a second season of WHA hockey, it quickly became business as usual for the Howe family. At the start of their careers in Houston, both Mark and Marty had chosen to live at home. Since they were each working, Colleen decided they had to pay rent. She charged them $30 a week for room and board. They protested at first, but she said it was either that or they could foot the family's grocery bill. They quickly opted for rent, which was a prudent financial decision. From the time he was little, Marty spent so much time staring into the fridge you'd think he was trying to keep the whole neighborhood air-conditioned. We used to joke that he ate only one meal a day, but it lasted from the time he woke up until he went to sleep.

In my career with the Wings I was always one for routine, and that didn't change when we moved to Texas. On game days, I still found that protein helped to settle my stomach. My boys took after their old man. Our big meal of the day would come around 1 P.M. The usual menu included either a sixteen-ounce porterhouse steak or a New York strip. I was a big fan of the beef in Texas. Colleen thought I was trying to compensate for a lifetime of living elsewhere by eating as much red meat as possible once I arrived in cattle country. For sides, we had cottage cheese, pears, and peaches with mayo, as well as the Howe family's special salad. Dessert was either Jell-O or ice cream, depending on how my weight was doing. I'm sure my pregame meal wouldn't be right for many players, but it worked well for me through the years. The rest of my game-day ritual included a mid-afternoon nap, which I'd take until around 5 P.M. After getting up, I'd dress, drink some tea with honey, and make my way to the rink. I did the same thing with few variations for more than twenty-five years. I found that being a creature of habit helped me focus on the game at hand instead of spending my energy worrying about other decisions.

As a player, I wasn't the most superstitious guy in the dressing room, but I wasn't the least superstitious either. Driving to the arena in Detroit, I'd try to hit green lights all the way to the Olympia. If I could make it without stopping, I considered it a good omen. I was also particular about my sticks. I used Northland sticks, which had three stripes wrapped around the shaft just above the blade. If I scored a goal with a certain stick or even if I just liked it, I'd remove one of the stripes. I'd tell everyone that if they wanted to take one of my sticks, to be sure to leave the good ones. For a time, I also had lucky undershorts. If I wore the shorts and we won, I'd put them away and wear them the next game. It's one habit I broke myself of, for obvious reasons. I eventually started buying them all in one color, so I wouldn't know which ones were the winning shorts. I don't know if any of those little rituals helped me on the ice, but I know one thing for certain: They didn't hurt.

My experience in both the NHL and the WHA meant that I used to get asked how the leagues stacked up against each other. The way I saw it, the NHL's big advantage was depth. Up and down the roster, NHL clubs had more guys who were able to play at a high level. Although NHL players were, on average, bigger, smarter, and faster, the WHA wasn't exactly full of scrubs. The top guys in the new league would have been stars in the NHL. In fact, there were NHL stars who went to the WHA, and WHA stars who went the other way. When the two leagues went head to head, the WHA actually performed quite well. The cumulative record ended up being 34–22–7 in favor of the WHA. Exhibition games aren't the same as the real thing, but it does show that the WHA was far from devoid of talent. Critics used to question how good the league could be when one of its best players was in his mid-forties. I didn't have much to say about that other than to point out that Number 9's track record in the NHL wasn't too bad either. Taking on an established league from scratch was no easy feat, but the WHA almost pulled it off. After all, the NHL owners wouldn't have worked so hard to quash it if the new league wasn't seen as a real threat.

When I look back at our team in Houston, I still think it was a heck of a squad. Our defense was definitely NHL caliber. Mark, for one, ended up playing sixteen years in the NHL and was inducted into the Hall of Fame in 2011. John Tonelli won four Stanley Cups and was selected to multiple All-Star teams. Marty went on to play 646 games as a professional, nearly 200 of which were in the NHL. I stand by the belief that the Aeros would have been among the top six or eight clubs in the NHL if given the chance. What we might have lacked in talent, we made up for in chemistry. The guys in the locker room trusted one another, which counts for a lot. In our four seasons in Houston between 1973 and 1977, we ended up winning a pile of games. Along with finishing first in our division four years in a row, we added a second consecutive Avco Cup to our trophy case in 1974–75. The time I spent in Houston also included a good run on the score sheet. I followed up my 100-point debut season with totals of 99 and 102. In my final year with the Aeros, injuries cost me 18 games and I finished with 68 points.

The early years in Houston with Marty and Mark were some of the most fun I'd ever had playing hockey. It made my comeback decision feel like a no-brainer. Of course, nothing lasts forever. In the final year of our contract, ownership of the Aeros changed hands. The new group was on shaky financial footing from the start and we started to worry that the club would follow some of the other franchises into bankruptcy. As good as things had been in Houston, they were definitely taking a turn for the worse. Colleen started exploring our options and, of all things, a return to the NHL looked like it could be in the cards.

There was a chance we might have ended up in Boston, which held the rights to Mark, or even back in Detroit. The Wings had traded for Marty's rights and the club liked the idea of bringing the Howes back into the fold. We liked it as well. Regardless of how things had turned out toward the end, Detroit was part of our DNA. I never stopped appreciating the fans or loving the city, and a homecoming would have been better than a dream. As can happen, however, business and egos got in the way. Ted Lindsay took over as the team's general manager while we were negotiating with the club. He made it pretty clear that a reunion wasn't on his agenda. A deal that would have put the three of us in Boston was also scuttled at the eleventh hour, when the team's owner balked at some of the guarantees included in our contract.

Throughout all of the back and forth with the NHL clubs, the New England Whalers had been sitting patiently in the wings. They'd let us know that if things didn't work out with Detroit or Boston, they had three lockers with our names on them waiting for us in Connecticut. After our deal with the Bruins fell apart, Colleen called Howard Baldwin, the president of the Whalers, and he was on the next plane to see us with a contract in hand. We arrived in

Hartford in 1977 for another season of WHA hockey. We liked Connecticut so much we stayed there for the next fifteen years.

Our time in New England also overlapped with an eventful period for hockey. In 1979, the NHL finally succeeded in ridding itself of its competitor through a merger with the WHA. Four teams ended up joining the league in the 1979–80 season: the Edmonton Oilers, the Winnipeg Jets, the Quebec Nordiques, and the New England Whalers, which changed its name to the Hartford Whalers due to pressure from the Bruins. After two years of retirement and six in the WHA, I found myself once again playing hockey in the NHL.

My final year in Hartford was memorable. The minute we took the ice, Mark, Marty, and I became the first father–son combination to suit up together in an NHL game. By that time, three of my four kids were married and two of them had children. Mark and his wife, Ginger, had our first grandchild, Travis, in 1978. We were playing in Edmonton on the night it happened. I scored a goal, which marked my first as a grandfather. Cathy had our second grandchild, Jaime, in October of the following year. By then, when my younger teammates would refer to me as "Grampa," I didn't have much of a comeback. (Interestingly, though the guys called me "Grampa," I never answered to "Dad." In our first few practices together in Houston, I think Marty and Mark were confused when I didn't respond to their calls on the ice. They soon figured out why and shifted from calling me "Dad" to "Gordie" just like everyone else. I thought that was the way it had to be. On a winning team there can't be any divisions. To this day, Marty still calls me by my first name.) Between our four children, Colleen and I eventually ended up with nine grandkids.

Fortunately, I wasn't the only one sporting some gray hairs. A mid-season trade with Winnipeg had brought forty-one-year-old Bobby Hull to Hartford. One night our coach, Don Blackburn, put us together on a line with Dave Keon, who was also in his early forties. I think we still hold the distinction of being the oldest line in hockey history. We were playing in Toronto, where Davey had starred for the Leafs in his prime. Not a bad line. We scored a couple of goals, which must have just killed Harold Ballard. I think the three of us actually chased the old man out of his booth that night.

In February 1980, Scotty Bowman decided to add me to his team for the league's All-Star game. It was being played in Detroit, and he thought I should be there. Scotty, who was behind the bench for Buffalo at the time, surely recognized that I was past my all-star days as a player, but as coach of the Prince of Wales Conference squad he had the prerogative to pick who he wanted. He took some heat for the choice, but he stuck to his guns. I can still remember the announcer calling the lineups that night. When my turn came around, he just called out, "Number 9." The standing ovation from the crowd for my twenty-third All-Star Game appearance seemed to last forever. If Detroit fans consider you to be one of their own, they'll stick with you through thick and thin. It didn't matter that my hair was gray and I was playing for the Whalers, to them I was still Gordie Howe of the Detroit Red Wings. Standing on the ice that night was not only one of the great moments I enjoyed in the game of hockey but also one of the best feelings I've ever had in my life. I was able to thank Scotty Bowman for it, but I wish I could have thanked each of the 21,000 fans there as well.

By the time I hung up my skates for good at the end of the 1979–80 season, I'd just finished my thirty-second season of professional hockey. I was fifty-two years old. When I say it out loud, it almost seems unreal that I played in five different decades. At the time, however, it seemed completely natural. When winter arrived, it always just felt like time to put on my skates. It didn't matter whether I was a kid or a grandfather, those feelings didn't change. Over more than three decades of professional hockey, I scored 801 goals in the NHL and added another 174 in the WHA for a total of 975. I amassed 1383 assists, 1049 in the NHL and 334 in the WHA. With 1850 points in the NHL and 508 in my six WHA seasons, I ended up with a career total of 2358 points. Over those years, I also spent more than 2000 minutes in the penalty box (a handful of which I probably even deserved).

My career, though, feels like much more than just a collection of numbers. It's playing for the fans and my teammates, and all of the friendships Colleen and I made over the years. It's being part of something bigger than just myself. It's being on the ice, sweating and bleeding with the boys. It's the wonderful life that hockey allowed me to give my family. It's a game I love. When I'm asked how I was able to play for so long, my answer is always the same: I never stopped loving the game. As the decades passed, my life saw a lot of changes—everyone's does—but that remained constant.

Looking back at it all, the words I shared with the fans in 1959 during my appreciation night keep running through my head: It's a long way from Saskatoon. No one could ask for a better ride.

# AFTERWORD

## MARTY, MARK, AND
## MURRAY HOWE
## AND CATHY PURNELL

A s kids going to school in Detroit, our teachers used to pass out a newspaper called *My Weekly Reader*. One day, when Murray was about six or seven, he opened his copy of *My Weekly Reader* and found a story about Dad. Excited to see a classmate's father featured in such a prestigious publication, the other kids started to pepper Murray with questions. He didn't have any answers, though. He knew that Dad played hockey for a living, but he never thought that was out of the ordinary. With the indignation that only a young child can muster, he rushed home after school to confront our parents. What made Dad so special that someone would write about him? How long had this been going on? Why had he not been informed of all of this sooner? In his typical fashion, Dad handled the questions in stride. He said it must have been a slow news week and they couldn't find anything else to write about. Then he probably went outside and mowed the lawn. That was Murray's introduction to the idea that our dad was famous.

We've all been asked what it was like being raised by arguably the world's best-known hockey player, but we doubt anyone finds our answers too satisfying. We didn't realize that our father was famous, because he just seemed like a normal dad. Other than being away a lot during the winter, he did the same things as every other parent on our block. That's what we thought as kids, anyway. As adults, we realize that we were wrong. He *is* different—a lot different. That difference just doesn't have anything to do with hockey.

If Dad has a selfish bone in his body, the four of us have yet to see it. That's not hyperbole, either. He's the most genuinely helpful person we've ever met. When he's at home, if he's not raking leaves, he's sweeping the floor or wiping down a countertop. At a gas station, after he finishes cleaning his own windshield, he doesn't think anything of moving over to the next car and cleaning it as well. It's not like he has nervous energy to burn off. You only have to watch him skate to know that he's as laid-back as they come. Rather, he just feels compelled to do nice things for people all the time. It's in his nature. He's humble and patient and never complains about anything. The rest of us complain all the time, but not him. It's not how he was raised.

Growing up in Saskatoon during the 1930s put a stamp on his character that he's kept for his entire life. His childhood wasn't easy. Our grandmother brought up nine children by herself with basically no resources whatsoever. She led a completely selfless existence in which she put her kids' welfare ahead of her own. At that time, you had to be tough to survive and, boy, was she ever. She used to help us with jigsaw puzzles when we were kids and occasionally

Mark, who was around ten or eleven at the time, would feel brave and challenge her to an arm wrestle. He was strong for a kid his age and she must have been in her sixties, but it didn't matter to her. She'd get down on the floor and pin his arm as quickly as he put it up there. For his part, Grandpa Albert was also as tough as they come. You couldn't be a shrinking violet and still run gangs of relief workers, as he did, during the Depression. He taught a young Gordie not to back down from anything. If you did, then it would be your own fault when you took the worst of it. When you look at Dad, it's as if he turned out to be an exact composite of his parents.

Anyone who watched Gordie Howe play might wonder if we're talking about the same guy or if his kids are just trying to sugarcoat things. It's no secret that Dad is remembered as much for the stitches he handed out as he is for the goals he scored. We know that. The Gordie Howe hat trick is named after him for a reason. Our mother spent half of her marriage trying to understand the two sides of her husband, and we're not sure if even she had him figured out. How can someone who's so kind and soft-spoken at home become so remorseless once he puts on skates? It's a Jekyll-and-Hyde duality that's not easy to reconcile.

The way Dad saw it, as a professional hockey player his job was to win games. As it turned out, he was perfectly suited to the task because he wanted to win more than anyone you'll ever meet. He decided early in his career that to be successful in the NHL he'd need to give the opposition a reason to slow down when they came to get the puck. If that meant throwing an elbow or putting some lumber on a guy, then it seemed like fair game to him. After all, everyone in the NHL was being paid to be there, and the odd cut or bruise was just a cost of doing business. Ironically, it was the respect he had for other players that made him feel like he had a license to play as ruthlessly as he did. He wasn't mean-spirited or dirty; he just figured that a few stitches or a knock to the ribs didn't cause any real harm. If it gave him the extra split second he needed to make a play, then that was justification enough for him. In his mind, playing any other way would be shortchanging the team. Some people might not approve, but his tactics gave him the space he needed to operate for more than thirty years. There was definitely a method to his madness.

When Mark was playing in Philadelphia, Brad McCrimmon told him a story from his rookie year with the Bruins, about the first time he played against Dad. They went into the corner together and Brad came out with a nick over his eye that needed stitches. When he returned to the bench, his teammates asked what had happened. He said that Gordie's stick had popped up and caught him in the eye. It had been an accident, though, and Gordie had said he was sorry. All the guys started to laugh. They pointed to their own scars and told Brad that Gordie had apologized for this one and that one, too. That was Dad. He let everyone on the ice know they shouldn't get too close.

Years later, he passed on some of that wisdom to another of Mark's teammates. While in Philly to watch Mark one night, Dad noticed that one of the Flyers was having a tough time holding his ground in the slot. Every time Tim Kerr—a big guy at six foot three and 225 pounds—went to the front of the net, the other team would hammer him until he moved. After the game, Dad went up to Tim and asked if he'd do him a favor. In the next big televised game the Flyers played, he told Tim to drop his gloves and pop someone on the other team. Tim was as gentlemanly a player as you'll find, so he agreed only reluctantly and only because it was Gordie Howe doing the asking. The next time Dad was in the arena, Tim hauled off and leveled a guy for no reason. The rest of the league must have been watching, because Tim suddenly found himself with more leeway. His soft hands deserve most of the credit for scoring more than 50 goals in each of the next four seasons, but Gordie's advice couldn't have hurt.

On the ice, our dad had an uncanny awareness of what was going on around him at all times. If he saw something that upset his sense of right and wrong—and if the officials weren't handling it—he didn't mind taking matters into his own hands. While playing in San Diego when he was in the WHA, he noticed one of the fans being a jackass. At the time, the arena had fencing instead of Plexiglas above the boards, and when a Houston player went into the corner, this fan would try to kick him in the head through the fence. Before a face-off in that end, Dad circled over to Marty and told him to pay attention. When the puck was dropped, he let himself get ridden into the corner where, sure enough, the fan was waiting to deliver a kick. It never landed. Somehow, the butt of Gordie's stick slipped through the mesh as he leaned back and popped the guy in the mouth, knocking him into the next row. The only reason Marty knew what had happened was because Dad had given him the heads-up. It happened so quickly he would have missed it otherwise.

We know that not everyone will approve of our dad's particular brand of frontier justice, but that's just how he's wired. He holds true to his own code, both on and off the ice. As a player, if someone disrespected his code, he didn't care how long it took to set things straight. A story from the mid-1960s shows just how long his memory could be. The Red Wings had missed the playoffs that year, so he'd picked up a gig as a television commentator for the postseason. On an off day, he wound up watching a bridge game between some of the players. Our dad was an avid bridge player and a real student of the game. At one point, Dick Duff, who played left wing for the Canadiens, took a trick by finessing a mediocre trump card past the other players. Appreciating the move, Dad mumbled, "Great play" under his breath. One of Montreal's defensemen, J.C. Tremblay, overheard him and snapped, "What would a dummy like you know about it?" That didn't sit well with Dad. He told J.C. to remember what he'd said and walked away. Six months later, the Red Wings were in Montreal to play the Canadiens. As it happened, it was the night that Dad scored his 600th goal. The fans had barely finished giving him a standing ovation for the achievement, when they reversed course and started to rain down boos. A few minutes after his big goal, Dad trailed J.C. into the corner after a puck. When he came out of the corner, he left J.C. on the ice with a fractured cheekbone. The Forum crowd didn't know why it had happened, but Dick Duff did. He skated past Gordie and said, "Card game." Dad just nodded.

Was his retribution excessive? An argument could be made that it was. On the other hand, J.C. might have done well to think twice before being so disrespectful. Our dad may not have been right all the time, but he was consistent. He hasn't changed to this day. Just last year he was signing autographs at the arena in Murray's hometown, when suddenly he stood up and walked purposefully toward a kid about thirty feet away. He had spotted the boy picking on his sister and didn't think that was right. He gently cuffed the kid on the back of the head and told him to smarten up. When the boy's family reached the front of the line, the boy's eyes were red and he was clearly sheepish. Taking the boy aside, Dad said that he needed to look out for his sister, not torment her. By the time they finished talking, the kid was beaming. We don't know how the boy's parents felt about their child getting lectured by Gordie Howe, but he couldn't help himself. His sense of justice is the same now as it was on the ice.

Lucky for us, our folks took a kinder, gentler approach to raising kids than was standard at the time. We're all still thankful for that, since getting spanked by Gordie Howe would have been no kind of fun. He has some of the biggest hands you've ever seen, with thick wrists to match. Really, he's just a big strong guy from head to toe. It's one of the reasons he was able to play hockey into his fifties. Athletically, he's not like most other people. His hand-eye coordination, for one, is almost supernatural. It doesn't matter what he's doing, he picks it up almost immediately. If he didn't find his calling in hockey, he probably would have ended up playing major league baseball or professional football. He was also a scratch golfer in his day. Put a club in his hand and he can swing it equally well from the left or right. Just name the sport and within a week he'll be playing it like he's been doing it his whole life.

It's been said that Dad was built to play hockey. There's actually more truth to that idea than anyone could know. When Mark was a teenager, he picked up the phone one day to find Eaton's on the other end of the line. They were tailoring some clothes for Dad and needed his measurements. Mark hustled upstairs to our parents' room and pulled a suit from the closet. When he measured the inseam, it was 27½ inches, which he knew must be wrong for someone six feet tall. He double-checked it, but the number stayed the same. After relaying the measurements to Eaton's, they asked him to measure the inseam yet again. Nothing changed. They told him they'd call back when his mother was home. Mark, of course, had been right. Few people realize it, but Dad's legs are remarkably short for such a big guy. Mark, for instance, is two inches shorter than Dad, yet his inseam is 32 inches. As it turned out, having short legs and a long torso was ideal for Dad's physical style of play. His low center of gravity made it nearly impossible to knock him off the puck. It's a physiological advantage that gave him an edge for his whole career. When it comes to playing hockey, it's as if he won the genetic lottery.

The other secret weapon that Dad had going for him that can't be overlooked was our mother. At the start of their marriage, she handled the household matters so he could focus on hockey. She paid the mortgage, called the plumber, talked to our schools, and did everything in between. When she took over as his business manager a few years later, it allowed him to sleep easy knowing that she was looking out for the family's best interests. Their personalities meshed perfectly. Our dad is so easygoing it can be astounding. He could be sitting in a hundred-degree room wearing a sweater and it wouldn't occur to him to complain. However, if someone came along and asked if he'd like to go somewhere to get a cold drink, he'd think that was a great idea. Well, our mom was always the person who came along. It made for an ideal team. He put all his energy into hockey and she worried about everything else. She was a born organizer. We used to joke that if the house caught fire, the first thing she'd go for would be her appointment book. It was like another child to her.

Once Dad finally hung up his skates for good, our parents might have been busier than when he was playing. They stayed in Connecticut for a few years before eventually moving back to Michigan. They decided to live in Traverse City, which is only about an hour away from a cabin we used to have on Bear Lake. It's a beautiful spot located on the Twin Bays of Lake Michigan. Dad loves being on the water, so it was perfect. Their post-hockey years were similar to those of a lot of retired folks. They golfed and fished and went to Florida for a couple of months every year. In addition, of course, they ran Howe Enterprises, which eventually became Power Play International. They did a lot of charity work, and Dad always had invites to attend card shows, golf tournaments, banquets, and other hockey-related events. The business of being Gordie Howe turned out to be a full-time job. In 1997, Dad also laced up for a shift with the Detroit Vipers of the International Hockey League. At nearly seventy years old, he became the first hockey player to play in a professional game in six different decades. Some dismissed it as a publicity stunt, but that didn't bother Dad, who just did it for fun. He still loved the game as much as ever and the idea of being back on the ice sounded too good to pass up. Our parents also stayed busy chasing after their nine grandchildren. Mark has three kids, Travis, Azia, and Nolan. Cathy has two, Jaime and Jade, and Murray has four, Meaghan, Gordie, Corey, and Sean. The oldest grandchildren now have kids of their own, which makes Dad a great-grandfather to Ainsley, Ella, Brenden, and Lahna.

Our parents took a lot of joy in watching their family grow. Unfortunately, not everything can be out of a storybook. We received some hard news in 2002 when Mum was diagnosed with a rare neurological illness called Pick's disease. She passed away in 2009. The WHA inducted her into its Hall of Fame a year later, along with Gordie, Marty, and Mark. Our dad misses her every day. We all do. Going through the last few years without her has been tough, especially on Dad. We know that he reminds himself often that they spent fifty-five very happy years together. He tells us that he feels lucky for every one of them. After Mum passed away, we realized that Dad would get pretty lonely on his own, so now he takes turns staying with all of us. And these past few years, he has needed someone nearby around the clock. Marty makes up a schedule and Dad rotates between each of our houses. It works well for everyone and means that the grandchildren, and now sometimes even the great-grandchildren, get to spend a lot of quality time with their grandpa. We do, too.

We cherish our time with Gordie all the more these past few years as it has become clear he has been dealing with cognitive impairment, a form of dementia. It has been a very slow decline over many years, though it has become more noticeable recently. His memory just isn't what it once was. At eighty-six, Gordie is becoming frail for the first time in his life. It is sad to see him struggle at things we all take for granted, things he wouldn't have given a second thought only a short time ago.

But even in adversity, Gordie can't resist helping. He has been involved in fundraising since Colleen passed away from her fight with Pick's Disease, another form of dementia. He works with the NHL Alumni in Toronto, Vancouver, and Calgary to raise funds for research and care for dementia and Alzheimer's patients and their families. He will continue this as long as he is capable.

That's Gordie. He has always enjoyed working and helping others. God bless the kindest, most giving person you ever had the pleasure of meeting. Mark, Cathy, Murray, and I are lucky to have had two such great parents and we miss our mother Colleen almost as much as Gordie misses the love of his life. We enjoy and cherish the time we have left with our father, and look forward to a few more fishing trips.

A peek into our house when we were growing up wouldn't have given any indication that the most famous hockey player in the world lived there. The trappings of fame were of no interest to him, and he rarely read his own press clippings. Around 1963, however, something came along that was hard to avoid. A group called Big Bob and the Dollars put out a novelty song called "Gordie Howe (Is the Greatest of Them All)" that became something of an improbable hit. For a while, it was all over local radio in Detroit, which gave us plenty of chances to tease our aw-shucks dad. It's an upbeat ditty with a chorus that went something like: *You can have your choice of all the rest / If you're a Howe fan, you've got the very best.* As many times as we laughed after hearing it on the radio, a funny thing has happened as we've grown up. The song still makes us smile, but now we realize that Big Bob and the Dollars may actually be right. It just doesn't have anything to do with hockey.

*Marty Howe*
*Mark Howe*
*Cathy Purnell*
*Murray Howe*

# CAREER STATISTICS AND RECORDS

| Year | Team | League | Regular Season | | |
|------|------|--------|----|----|----|
| | | | GP | G | A |
| 1944–45 | Galt Red Wings | OHA | — | — | — |
| 1945–46 | Omaha Knights | USHL | 51 | 22 | 25 |
| 1946–47 | Detroit Red Wings | NHL | 58 | 7 | 15 |
| 1947–48 | Detroit Red Wings | NHL | 60 | 16 | 28 |
| 1948–49 | Detroit Red Wings | NHL | 40 | 12 | 25 |
| 1949–50 | Detroit Red Wings | NHL | 70 | 35 | 33 |
| 1950–51 | Detroit Red Wings | NHL | 70 | 43 | 43 |
| 1951–52 | Detroit Red Wings | NHL | 70 | 47 | 39 |
| 1952–53 | Detroit Red Wings | NHL | 70 | 49 | 46 |
| 1953–54 | Detroit Red Wings | NHL | 70 | 33 | 48 |
| 1954–55 | Detroit Red Wings | NHL | 64 | 29 | 33 |
| 1955–56 | Detroit Red Wings | NHL | 70 | 38 | 41 |
| 1956–57 | Detroit Red Wings | NHL | 70 | 44 | 45 |
| 1957–58 | Detroit Red Wings | NHL | 64 | 33 | 44 |
| 1958–59 | Detroit Red Wings | NHL | 70 | 32 | 36 |
| 1959–60 | Detroit Red Wings | NHL | 70 | 28 | 45 |
| 1960–61 | Detroit Red Wings | NHL | 64 | 23 | 49 |
| 1961–62 | Detroit Red Wings | NHL | 70 | 33 | 44 |
| 1962–63 | Detroit Red Wings | NHL | 70 | 38 | 48 |
| 1963–64 | Detroit Red Wings | NHL | 69 | 26 | 47 |
| 1964–65 | Detroit Red Wings | NHL | 70 | 29 | 47 |
| 1965–66 | Detroit Red Wings | NHL | 70 | 29 | 46 |
| 1966–67 | Detroit Red Wings | NHL | 69 | 25 | 40 |
| 1967–68 | Detroit Red Wings | NHL | 74 | 39 | 43 |
| 1968–69 | Detroit Red Wings | NHL | 76 | 44 | 59 |
| 1969–70 | Detroit Red Wings | NHL | 76 | 31 | 40 |
| 1970–71 | Detroit Red Wings | NHL | 63 | 23 | 29 |
| 1973–74 | Houston Aeros | WHA | 70 | 31 | 69 |
| 1974–75 | Houston Aeros | WHA | 75 | 34 | 65 |
| 1975–76 | Houston Aeros | WHA | 78 | 32 | 70 |
| 1976–77 | Houston Aeros | WHA | 62 | 24 | 44 |
| 1977–78 | New England Whalers | WHA | 76 | 34 | 62 |
| 1978–79 | New England Whalers | WHA | 58 | 19 | 24 |
| 1979–80 | Hartford Whalers | NHL | 80 | 15 | 26 |
| | NHL Totals | | 1,767 | 801 | 1,049 |
| | WHA Totals | | 419 | 174 | 334 |
| | Major League Totals | | 2,186 | 975 | 1,383 |
| | Regular & Playoff Totals | | 2,421 | 1,071 | 1,518 |

GP = Games Played, G = Goals, A = Assists, PTS = Points, PIM = Penalties in Minutes

| PTS | PIM | Playoffs | | | | |
|---|---|---|---|---|---|---|
| | | GP | G | A | PTS | PIM |
| — | — | — | — | — | — | — |
| 48 | 53 | 6 | 2 | 1 | 3 | 15 |
| 22 | 52 | 5 | 0 | 0 | 0 | 18 |
| 44 | 63 | 10 | 1 | 1 | 2 | 11 |
| 37 | 57 | 11 | 8 | 3 | 11 | 19 |
| 68 | 69 | 1 | 0 | 0 | 0 | 7 |
| 86 | 74 | 6 | 4 | 3 | 7 | 4 |
| 86 | 78 | 8 | 2 | 5 | 7 | 2 |
| 95 | 57 | 6 | 2 | 5 | 7 | 2 |
| 81 | 109 | 12 | 4 | 5 | 9 | 31 |
| 62 | 68 | 11 | 9 | 11 | 20 | 24 |
| 79 | 100 | 10 | 3 | 9 | 12 | 8 |
| 89 | 72 | 5 | 2 | 5 | 7 | 6 |
| 77 | 40 | 4 | 1 | 1 | 2 | 0 |
| 78 | 57 | — | — | — | — | — |
| 73 | 46 | 6 | 1 | 5 | 6 | 4 |
| 72 | 30 | 11 | 4 | 11 | 15 | 10 |
| 77 | 54 | — | — | — | — | — |
| 86 | 100 | 11 | 7 | 9 | 16 | 22 |
| 73 | 70 | 14 | 9 | 10 | 19 | 16 |
| 76 | 104 | 7 | 4 | 2 | 6 | 20 |
| 75 | 83 | 12 | 4 | 6 | 10 | 12 |
| 65 | 53 | — | — | — | — | — |
| 82 | 53 | — | — | — | — | — |
| 103 | 58 | — | — | — | — | — |
| 71 | 58 | 4 | 2 | 0 | 2 | 2 |
| 52 | 38 | — | — | — | — | — |
| 100 | 46 | 13 | 3 | 14 | 17 | 34 |
| 99 | 84 | 13 | 8 | 12 | 20 | 20 |
| 102 | 76 | 17 | 4 | 8 | 12 | 31 |
| 68 | 57 | 11 | 5 | 3 | 8 | 11 |
| 96 | 85 | 14 | 5 | 5 | 10 | 15 |
| 43 | 51 | 10 | 3 | 1 | 4 | 4 |
| 41 | 42 | 3 | 1 | 1 | 2 | 2 |
| 1,850 | 1,685 | 157 | 68 | 92 | 160 | 220 |
| 508 | 399 | 78 | 28 | 43 | 71 | 115 |
| 2,358 | 2,084 | 235 | 96 | 135 | 231 | 355 |
| 2,589 | 2,419 | | | | | |

# AWARDS

| | |
|---|---|
| Art Ross Trophy | 1950–51, 1951–52, 1952–53, 1953–54, 1956–57, 1962–63 (NHL leading scorer) |
| First All-Star Team Right Wing | 1950–51, 1951–52, 1952–53, 1953–54, 1956–57, 1957–58, 1959–60, 1962–63, 1965–66, 1967–68, 1968–69, 1969–70 |
| Hart Memorial Trophy | 1951–52, 1952–53, 1956–57, 1957–58, 1959–60, 1962-63 (MVP of the NHL) |
| Lester Patrick Trophy | 1966–67 (presented for outstanding service to hockey in the United States) |
| Second All-Star Team Right Wing | 1948–49, 1949–50, 1955–56, 1958–59, 1960–61, 1963–64, 1964–65, 1966–67 |
| Order of Canada | 1971 |
| Gary L. Davidson Trophy | 1972 (MVP of the WHA) |
| Inducted into the Hockey Hall of Fame | 1972 |
| NHL Lifetime Achievement Award | 2008 (inaugural recipient) |
| Inducted into the WHA Hall of Fame | 2010 (as a member of the Howe family) |

# ACKNOWLEDGMENTS

I owe a debt of gratitude to a number of people without whom this book would have stayed on the drawing board. My children, of course, always come first. Marty, Mark, Cathy, and Murray, thank you for making this project possible, as well as being the best kids anyone could ask for. As ever, I'd also like to thank my wife, Colleen, who brought so much happiness to my life in more than fifty years of marriage. I miss you, honey.

I'd also like to thank my parents, Albert and Katherine. So much of who I am, I owe to them.

This would be incomplete without a special thank you to a few people that should be acknowledged. Bill and Edna Gadsby have been life friends to Colleen and me. I still cherish their friendship in good times and sad. Ron Toigo and his family have been like extended family, and we look forward to our trips to Vancouver. Thanks too to Bill Dineen, who believed in me and brought Marty, Mark and myself to the Houston Aeros and fulfilled my dream of playing pro hockey alongside my sons.

# ACKNOWLEDGMENTS

I would like to thank Felix and Reta Gatt for everything. Felix has been so helpful to me and my family. A more positive person you'll never meet. Finally, Bob Philpot and family. I have been fishing with Bob, his grandfather, father and friends since the 50s. What wonderful people.

The coaches and teachers I've had over the years also deserve a special thank you. Without their support, kids like me would never make it to the NHL.

A sincere thanks goes to Paul Haavardsrud, who helped to take the thoughts in my head and put them down on paper. I appreciate the dedication, skill, and hard work it took to bring my story to these pages. This book also wouldn't have happened without Nick Garrison and his team at Penguin. Without his determination and expertise this project would have remained an idea instead of becoming a reality.

Finally I would like to offer a thank you to all the hockey fans I have encountered while at the arena but more so in my everyday walk of life. Whether at the rink, a public appearance, crossing paths at an airport, or just a brief encounter while having breakfast at the local diner, every interaction brings a warmth and kindness with it. I thank you all for the kind words, the smiles, hugs and laughter. Hopefully I have enriched your lives as much as you have enriched mine.

# INDEX

# INDEX

# INDEX

# INDEX